I0032932

2ND EDITION

Economic Citizenship

by Jay Butler

AssetProtectionServices.com

ISBN 978-0-9914644-4-9

ECONOMIC CITIZENSHIP

CONTRIBUTION • NATURALIZATION • REAL PROPERTY

Table of **Contents**

Disclaimer

Asset Protection Services of America

The inverted "V" displayed on our shield is the uppercase letter "L" in ancient Greek identifying the people of Lacedaemonia, which in historical times was the proper name for the Spartan state. The Greek cry "Molõn Labé" means "Come and Get Them" as spoken by King Leonidas in response to the Persian army's demand for the outnumbered Spartans (300 against 300,000) to surrender their weapons during battle in the narrow pass or 'hot gates' of Thermopylae in 480 B.C. The iconic expression has become a symbol of courage to defend that which belongs to you, even if faced against overwhelming or insurmountable odds.

Author

Jay Butler is the Managing Director of Asset Protection Services of America, the former Managing Director of Asset Protection Services International, Ltd and the former Vice-President of Sales and Marketing for Corporate Support Services of Nevada Inc. Mr. Butler holds a Bachelor's Degree of Fine Arts from Boston University.

Jay has provided customized business entity structuring for clients in all 50 states along with some of the most respected names in the industry including the Jay Mitton organization "the father of asset protection" and Real Estate Investor Association seminars.

While working with Wealth Protection Concepts, LLC under the tutelage of the former Las Vegas and North Las Vegas city attorney Carl E. Lovell Jr. (now deceased from Leukemia), Mr. Butler was bestowed the title of "Asset Protection Planner" for his competency and experience. He also co-authored the first edition of his book "Cover Your Assets: Legal Authorities on Asset Protection, Tax Strategies and Estate Planning" © 2006 with Dr. Lovell.

While residing in Switzerland, Mr. Butler was the Associate Director of "CO-Handelszentrum GmbH" providing Swiss company formation and administration services and executed a full-range of fiduciary responsibilities including sales, client support and international corporate compliance services (KYC, FATCA, AML, FATF and Swiss Code of Obligations).

Jay builds his relationships through consistent attention to detail and reliable support. He has traveled extensively throughout the United States (having visited 49 of the 50 states), explored 36 nations worldwide, and has lived in a total of 7 countries throughout North America, Central America, the Middle East, North Africa and Europe.

Dr Robert Hagopian is semi-retired and the former CEO of Nevada Trustee Services Group Inc, which has provided trustee services to attorneys and law firms throughout the United States since 2005, and the former CEO of the Commerce Bank Ltd in Hong Kong.

Since 1968, Robert has traveled extensively throughout Asia and lived in Japan, Hong Kong and the Philippines with current residency and offices in Manilla.

Dr. Hagopian holds a Bachelor of Science (BS) degree in business administration, an MsD (doctorate) in philosophy and a "jure Dignitatis" Bachelor of Laws degree.

Since 1984, Dr. Hagopian has been structuring business entities for optimum wealth preservation, profitability, asset protection and limiting personal liability through the use of domestic corporations, limited liability companies and various trust vehicles.

Robert has developed innovative processes for the acquisition, holding and marketing of real property. In 2008, Dr. Hagopian applied for the patent-pending "Equity Recovery Program". Based on IRC 351 rules for the transference of real estate to a corporation, the program lawfully avoids capital gains tax, self-employment and state taxes upon the sale of real property.

Contact Us

Please browse our website at www.AssetProtectionServices.com and contact us to schedule your free private asset protection consultation. We welcome the opportunity to hold a 3-way conference call with your tax advisor and/or legal counsel to address any specific questions or concerns you may have. Experience has demonstrated it favorable to have all related parties "on the same page" when creating your structure.

Asset Protection Services of America
701 South Carson Street (Suite #200)
Carson City, Nevada 89701-5239
Office   (775) 461-5255
Skype   Jay_Butler
E-Mail   info@AssetProtectionServices.com
Website   www.AssetProtectionServices.com

Books by Jay Butler
and Dr. Robert Hagopian

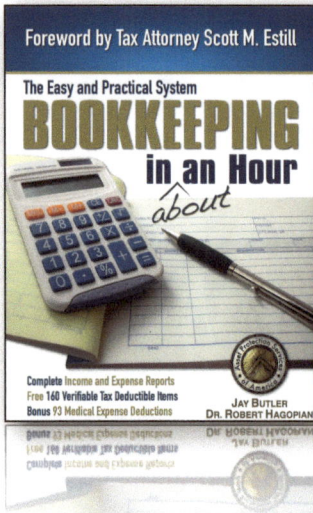
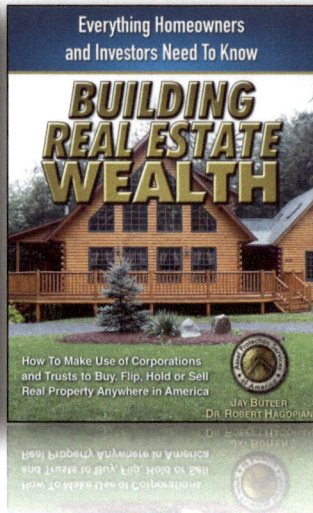
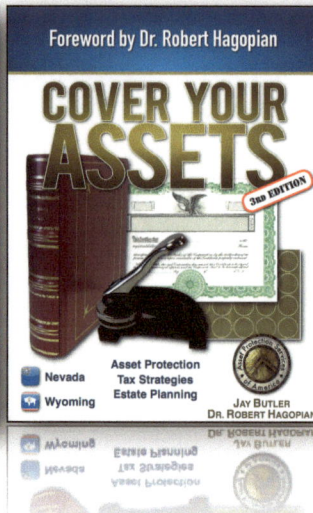
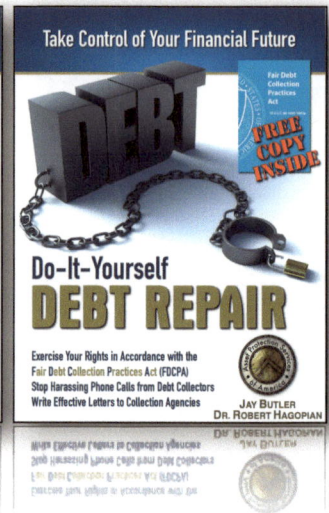

Bookkeeping in About an Hour	ISBN 978-0-9914644-0-1
Building Real Estate Wealth	ISBN 978-0-9914644-1-8
Cover Your Assets *(3rd Edition)*	ISBN 978-0-9914644-2-5
Do-It-Yourself Debt Repair	ISBN 978-0-9914644-7-0

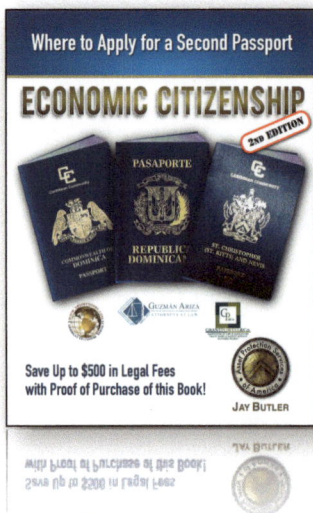
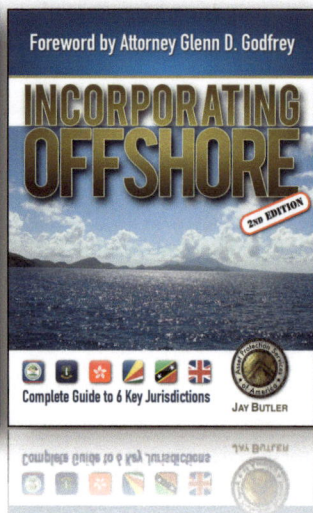
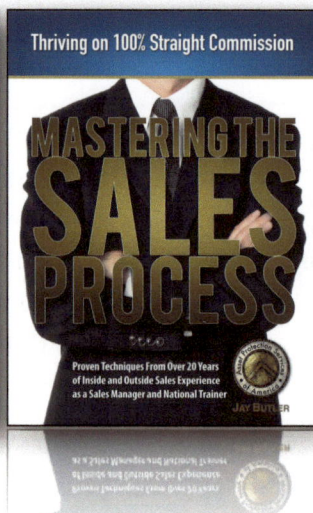
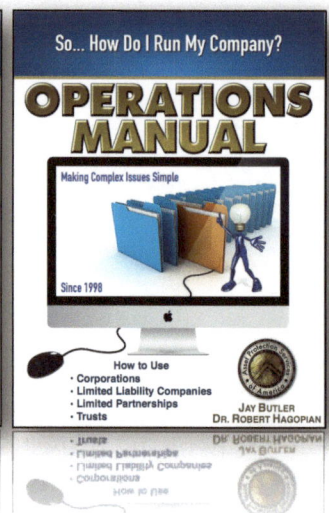

Economic Citizenship *(2nd Edition)*	ISBN 978-0-9914644-4-9
Incorporating Offshore *(2nd Edition)*	ISBN 978-0-9914644-5-6
Mastering the Sales Process	ISBN 978-0-9914644-6-3
Operations Manual	ISBN 978-0-9914644-3-2

Obtaining and Renewing Your Passport

The United States government is aggressively denying citizens their constitutional right to receive and renew their passports. Through long-form applications (which are virtually impossible to complete) and claims of unpaid state or federal income taxes (which are virtually impossible to disprove) Americans are quickly finding themselves unable to leave the country.

Whether you've been awake for years or sense 'like a splinter in your mind' that something is inherently wrong with society, the instincts driving you to prepare for tomorrow's challenges today are correct. If a financial collapse of the United States concerns you or if you wish to secure a location where your family can live and work in the event of civil unrest, then it is time to act on your intuition!

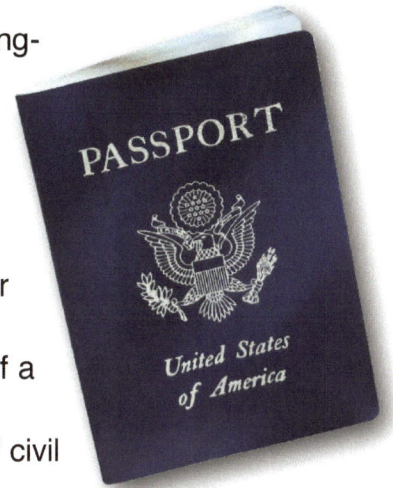

Advantages of a Second Passport

Advantages to holding a second passport (or dual citizenship) include the ability to:

1.) Leave the country in the event of civil unrest;
2.) Travel internationally with greater anonymity to nations which are not hospitable toward your (home) country;
3.) Open certain types of offshore bank accounts and investment funds;
4.) Reduce or eliminate various forms of taxation;
5.) Further protect assets, including precious metals, commodities and real property;
6.) Securely hold ownership to offshore instruments;
7.) Permanently live and work in the foreign country wherein the dual citizenship is held or is recognized by a neighboring or participating jurisdiction.
8.) If you so wish, permanently renounce your U.S. citizenship. (Such an option is at your sole discretion and is *not* a requirement for dual citizenship in most countries.)

Be attentive to on-going tax consequences, as holding citizenship in one jurisdiction may not preclude you from owing taxes in another jurisdiction. Tax Information Exchange Agreements (TIEA) discourage tax avoidance between signatory countries, however there are Double Taxation Avoidance Agreements (DTAA) to help mitigate this among participating nations.

Dual citizenship can provide you with the key to a more relaxed international traveling experience, open doors to a world of possibility for new personal and business relationships, investment opportunities, financial security and individual freedoms!

Naturalization

Naturalization is the method by which an individual, couple or family can obtain citizenship in a foreign jurisdiction by means of a 'naturalization process' which sometimes requires applicants to reside in the country during the entire application process. Most countries offer citizenship by some form of "naturalization" including, but not limited to, Belize, Costa Rica, the Dominican Republic, Ecuador, Panama and Paraguay.

To best answer the question "What are the least expensive countries in which to obtain dual citizenship?" the answer would rely heavily on whether you have the financial means to afford an 'economic citizenship' program or the time to wait for a 'naturalization' program to come to fruition. Generally speaking, economic citizenship programs make second passports available within 3 to 12 months while naturalization programs can take 3 to 7 years.

If the case is the latter, then prices and residency or visitation requirements can vary dramatically. Although your options are more abundant for naturalization programs so too is the demand for thorough research before making a decision. Unfortunately the length of this book will not permit for a comprehensive answer to the least expensive countries in which to obtain dual citizenship by way of naturalization. Please contact us to schedule a private consultation to get more details on a naturalization program in additional jurisdictions.

Legal Foundation

Regardless of which jurisdiction best meets your needs, you must be pointed to the specific underlying legal foundation upon which the dual citizenship program (whether naturalization or economic) is being made available to the public. Meaning, if you are not provided with a section from the constitution, a constitutional amendment or piece of current legislation validating the program is available to the public then you are likely to become involved in a scam.

Be leery of anyone who tries to sell you a second passport based on adoption, the death of a citizen, or 'special activities' such as an involvement in the film industry or private security, etc. The use of a fraudulent passport is a serious international crime and punishable with long prison sentences in most every country.

Whomever you choose to provide your dual citizenship services, the actual work should be performed by legal counsel on-the-ground in the country wherein you are seeking your second citizenship. There are a number of con-artists seeking to charge $25,000 to $50,000 for passports without utilizing any legal assistance. Under no circumstances whatsoever should you consider attempting to procure a second passport without competent and reliable legal counsel located on-the-ground in the country wherein you wish to hold dual citizenship.

Economic Citizenship

Economic Citizenship is the method by which an individual, couple or family can obtain citizenship in a foreign jurisdiction by means of an economic investment into such country by way of charitable contribution, purchase of real property or financial investment into some form of business, commercial activity or financial instrument.

Currently there are around a half-dozen other countries in the world which offer a legal means of obtaining dual citizenship through economic investment. The focus of this publication is to assist clients interested in obtaining dual citizenship beginning at $100,000 to $250,000 (USD). Alphabetically, here is a list of the most well-known countries which currently offer second passports through some form of economic citizenship program:

	Jurisdiction	Cost	Time to Citizenship
1.)	Commonwealth of Dominica	$ 100,000+ (USD)	2 - 3 Months
2.)	Dominican Republic	$ 200,000+ (USD)	12 - 18 Months
3.)	St Kitts & Nevis	$ 250,000+ (USD)	4 - 6 Months
4.)	Antigua & Barbuda	$ 250,000+ (USD)	Coming Soon!
5.)	Ireland	€ 500,000 - € 2 Million+ (EURO)	5 Years
6.)	New Zealand	$ 1.25 Million+ (USD)	4 Years
7.)	Austria	€ 3 - 4 Million+ (EURO)	1 - 1.5 Years
8.)	Cyprus	€ 3 - 5 Million+ (EURO)	5 Years
9.)	United Kingdom	£ 200,000 - £ 1 Million+ (GBP)	5 Years

**Save Up to $500 on Legal Fees
with Proof of Purchase of this Book!**

Save up to $500 on your legal fees with 'proof of purchase' of this book! The fees described in this publication are determined solely by our legal providers and we do not charge so much as $1 more for any services mentioned herein. However, by purchasing this publication, our legal providers have agreed to provide you with up to $500 in savings on legal fees when obtaining your dual citizenship! Please contact our offices for more details.

Belize

The Belize Citizenship by Naturalization program is a straight-forward process. Upon entering Belize, individuals may secure a work visa and shall be eligible to apply for residency after remaining in Belize for a period of one year. (Belize immigration fees for permanent residence permits vary based on the applicant's current country of citizenship.) Then, after having lived in Belize for a total of five years, individuals are eligible for naturalization and may apply for citizenship and a passport. The Belize Citizenship by Naturalization program is not available to Indian nationals or Asian nationals.

About Belize

Activities

Belize is an outdoor enthusiast's playground with snorkeling, scuba diving, surfing, wind sailing, kayaking, canoeing, biking, hiking, cave exploring, river tubing, white-water rafting, jungle expeditions, fishing, bird watching, deep mountain forest camping and more. The Belize Barrier Reef has been named one of the "Seven Wonders of the Underwater World" by CEDAM International and Belize is home to ancient Mayan temples as well as some of the most exotic plant, animal and trees species on the planet.

Climate

Belize has a tropical Caribbean climate that is warm, humid and controlled in large part by the Atlantic trade winds. Along the coastline, temperatures average around 22°C in January and 25°C in July. As the trade winds loose strength moving inland, the mainland areas will see summer temperatures in excess of 38°C. The dry season is the most attractive time of year for tourists and generally runs from December through May. The rainy season extends from June through November and brings varying amounts of precipitation. The Corozal District in the north may only see 50 cm of rain, while Punta Gorda to the south may see in excess of 170 cm per annum. Notwithstanding the heavy wind, rain and flooding from a passing hurricane, Belize has consistent weather patterns.

Culture

Belize is the most sparsely populated country in Central America. Despite a majority of the citizenry being 18 years of age or younger, Belize possesses an impressive 94% literacy rate. The country is multi-cultural with resident ethnic groups such as the Mestizo, Creole, Mayan, Caribe and Garifuna. Belizians have one of the highest birth rates in the worlds, with an average of four children per family and a life expectancy of 68.3 years. The predominant religion in Belize is Christianity with Roman Catholics and Protestants making up the two primary denominations. Belize is unique in Central and South America in that English is the official language. This fact makes international business and tourism favorable for attracting many Americans, Canadians and Europeans to Belize.

Economy and Offshore Financial Services

Belize is a member of the British Commonwealth, United Nations, WTO, IMF and other international organizations. The Queen of England is the head of state and formally represented in Belize by the Governor General. The national assembly, comprised of the house of representatives and the senate, carries out the duties of the legislative branch of the Belizian parliamentary democracy. The executive branch is overseen by the government and the prime minister. Belize is divided into 6 administrative districts; Belize, Cayo, Corozal, Orange Walk, Stan Creek and Toledo. Belize is known for its exports of tropical agrarian products including bananas, citrus, fish, sugar and timber. Belize has a very long 6 month tourist season attracting hundreds of thousands of people from around the world. The Belize International Business Companies Act in 1990 has steadily given rise to a strong financial offshore services economy. When Belize refused to cower to unjust pressure by the United States to reveal confidential client information, they eventually exonerated after years of international isolation as a respected member of the offshore financial services community. The primary commercial banks in Belize are the Alliance Bank, Atlantic Bank, Bank of Nova Scotia, Belize Bank and the First Caribbean International Bank. Asset Protection Services of America offers incorporation services for International Business Companies in Belize.

Geography

Belize is the northern most country in Central America. Located along the southeast part of the Yucatan peninsula, the entire east coast of Belize faces the Caribbean Sea. Belize is a seaside country spanning 280 kilometers from north to south and 105 kilometers from east to west. Much of the Hondo river creates a natural borderline between Belize and Mexico to the north and Guatemala to the west and south. The highest point in Belize is Victoria Peak standing 1,120 meters above sea level in the Maya Mountains. The Belize River, also known as the Old River, is the nation's largest and most historic waterway. Navigable up to the Guatemalan border, the Belize River allows for goods and services to be transported deep inland and gave rise to the name of Belize City, which is situated near the mouth of the trade route. Over 90% of Belize is saturated with virgin tropical rain forests, rich in flora, fauna and precious species of timber. Belize boasts hundreds of picturesque islands, islets, cayes, a 322 kilometer barrier reef (largest in the northern hemisphere and second largest in the world) and the biggest sinkhole on earth called the Blue Hole.

History

The ancient Mayan civilization inhabited Belize for centuries with a population at one point believed to exceed 400,000 people. Europeans came to know of modern day Belize City with the discovery by Christopher Columbus in 1502. Due to the resilience of the inland natives, it wasn't until 1786 that the British government was able to appoint a Quartermaster General representative to Belize for the first time. In 1862 Belize was officially declared a British Colony and was renamed "British Honduras" and continued under this name for more than 100 years. When the demand for internationally exported timber diminished in the twentieth century Belizians rose up and gained their independence as a nation in 1964. In 1973 the country renamed itself Belize and in 1980 the United Nations adopted a resolution recognizing Belize as an independent sovereign nation.

Interesting Facts

Capital
Belmopan

Population
333,200

Official Language
English

GDP
$2.651 Billion

Government
British Commonwealth
Parliamentary Democracy
Constitutional Monarchy

Currency
Belize Dollar (BZD)

Laws
Common Law

Driving
Right

Independence Day
September 21st, 1981

Internet
.bz

Total Area
22,966 Km2

Calling Code
+501

Belize
Citizenship by Naturalization

The Belize Citizenship by Naturalization program is a straight-forward process. Upon entering Belize, individuals may secure a work visa and shall be eligible to apply for residency after remaining in Belize for a period of one year. Belize immigration fees for permanent residence permits vary based on the applicant's current country of citizenship. *(See the Chart Below)* Then, after having lived in Belize for a total of five years, individuals are eligible for naturalization and may apply for citizenship and a passport. The Belize Citizenship by Naturalization program is not available to Indian nationals or Asian nationals.

Immigration Fees
$1 USD = $2 BZD

	Permanent Residence Permit	Duration	Fees
a	**Citizens of Central American countries, the Dominican Republic and Mexico** • Costa Rica • Dominican Republic • El Salvador • Guatemala • Honduras • Mexico • Nicaragua • Panama	Indefinite	$750 (BZD)
b	**Citizens of Caribbean Community (CARICOM) countries** • Antigua and Barbuda • Bahamas (not a member of the Common Market) • Barbados • Commonwealth of Dominica • Grenada • Guyana • Haiti • Jamaica • Montserrat • St Kitts and Nevis • Saint Lucia • St Vincent and the Grenadines • Suriname • Trinidad and Tobego	Indefinite	$500 (BZD)

	Permanent Residence Permit	Duration	Fees
c	**Citizens of the United States of America (USA), Cuba and South American countries (except Guyana)** • Argentina • Bolivia • Brazil • Chile • Columbia • Cuba • Ecuador • French Guiana • Paraguay • Peru • United States of America • Uruguay • Venezuela	Indefinite	$2,000 (BZD)
d	**Citizens of the People's Republic of China (PRC)**	Indefinite	$2,000 (BZD)
e	**Citizens of Bangladesh, Pakistan and Sri Lanka**	Indefinite	$5,000 (BZD)

	Permanent Residence Permit	Duration	Fees
f	**Citizens of other Commonwealth countries not included in any of the above categories** • Australia and Australian Antarctic Territory) • Botswana • British Antarctic and British Indian Ocean Territory • Brunei • Cameroon • Canada • Channel Islands • Cook Islands • Falkland Islands and Falkland Islands Dependencies • Fiji • Gambia • Ghana • Gibraltar • India • Isle of Man • Kenya • Kiribati • Lesotho • Malawi • Malaysia • Maldives • Malta • Mozambique • Namibia • Nauru • New Zealand • Nigeria • Niue • Norfolk Island • Papua New Guinea • Pitcairn Islands • Ross Dependency • Seychelles • Sierra Leone • Singapore • Solomon Islands • South Africa • St Helena • Swaziland • Tanzania • Tokelau • Tonga • Tuvalu • Uganda • Vanuatu • Western Samoa • Zambia • Zimbabwe	Indefinite	$1,500 (BZD)

	Permanent Residence Permit	Duration of Permit	Fees
g	**Citizens of European countries** • Member States of the European Union (EU) • Austria • Belgium • Bulgaria • Cyprus • Czech Republic • Denmark • Estonia • Finland • Germany • Greece • Hungary • Ireland • Italy • Latvia • Lithuania • Luxembourg • Malta • Netherlands • Poland • Portugal • Romania • Slovakia • Spain • Sweden • United Kingdom	Indefinite	$3,000 (BZD)
h	**Citizens of all other countries not included in categories (a) to (g) above**	Indefinite	$4,000 (BZD)

Citizenship by Naturalization

Residency Application*

- ✅ Statutory Due Diligence for Up to Two Persons
- ✅ Filing Residency Application
- ✅ Belize General 12.5% Sales Tax
- ✅ Government Application Fees *($150)*
- ✅ Government Program Fees *($1,000)*
- ✅ Government Card Fees *($200)*
- ✅ Application Time is 1 Business Day
- ❌ Any Applicable Immigration Fees *(Varies – See Previous Chart)*

Work Permit*

- ✅ Filing Work Permit Application
- ✅ Belize General 12.5% Sales Tax
- ✅ Government Application Fees *($1,125)*
- ✅ Government Expedite Fees *($900)*
- ✅ Application Time is 1 Business Day

* Legal Fees   Please contact our offices for specific details.

Belize
Qualified Retired Persons Program

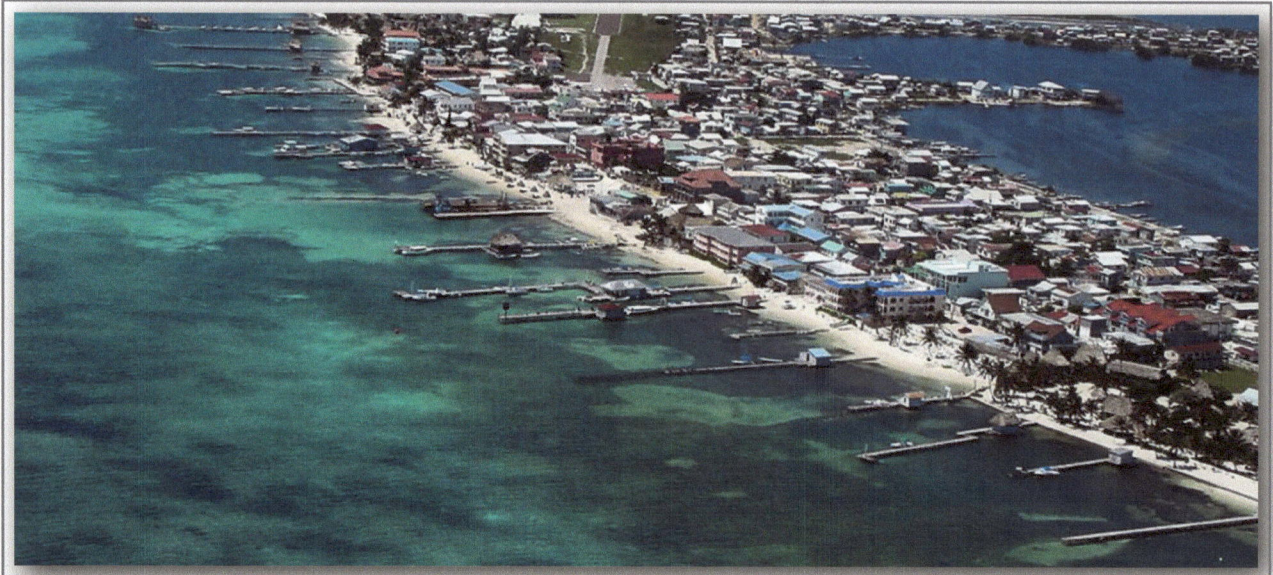

Introduction

The Belize Qualified Retired Persons (Incentives) Program was created especially for those people who wish to live in Belize and can prove a permanent and consistent income from investments abroad or in Belize, pensions or other retirement benefits. Anyone forty-five (45) years or older from anywhere in the world can qualify for the program. A person who qualifies can also include his or her dependents in the program. Dependents include spouses and children under the age of eighteen (18) or under the age of twenty-three (23) if enrolled in a university. Qualifying Applicants must provide documentation demonstrating a pension or annuity of a minimum of $2,000 (USD) per month or $24,000 (USD) per year.

Incentives

All persons who have been designated a Qualified Retired Person shall be entitled, on first entering Belize, to import his or her personal effects and an approved means of transportation free of all import duties and taxes. A Qualified Retired Person shall be exempt from the payment of all taxes and duties on all income or receipts which accrue to him or her from a source outside of Belize whether that income is generated from work performed or from an investment.

Application

Each application for the retirement program shall be processed by the Belize Tourism Board in collaboration with the Ministry of National Security and the Department of Immigration and Nationality. Persons interested in the program must submit completed applications to the Belize Tourism Board with the following supporting documentation. Dependents should submit all documents listed with exception of the proof of income.

1. Birth Certificate - A copy of a certificate for the applicant and each dependent.

2. Marriage Certificate - (if married and spouse is a dependent)

3. Authentic Police Record - An authentic police record from the applicant's last place of residency issued within one month prior to this application.

4. Passport - Clear copies of complete passport (including all blank pages) of applicant and all dependents that have been certified by a Notary Public. The copies must have the passport number, name of principal, number of pages and the seal or stamp of the Notary Public.

5. Proof of Income - An official statement from a bank or financial institution certifying that the applicant is the recipient of a pension or annuity of a minimum of Two Thousand United States Dollars (US $2,000.00) per month.
    b. Financial Statement from a financial institution, bank, credit union or building society in Belize certifying that the applicant's investment or deposit will generate the sum, of a minimum of Two Thousand United States Dollars (US $2,000.00) per month or the equivalent of Twenty Four Thousand United States Dollars (US $24,000.00) per year.

6. Medical Examination - Applicants should undergo a complete medical examination including an AIDS test. A copy of the medical certificate must be attached to the application.

7. Photos - Four front and four-side passport size photographs that have been taken recently of applicant and dependents.

Income Sources

1. <u>Retired Pensioner</u> - A retired pensioner is that person who qualifies under the program and receives a monthly income of not less than US $2,000.00 through a pension or annuity that has been generated outside of Belize.

2. <u>Certification</u> -
   i)   When a company grants a pension, that company has to prove that it has been in operation for at least 20 years by submitting proof of registration.
   ii) The company that grants the pension shall certify that the pension of no less than US $2,000.00 per month will be forwarded to a reputable financial institution within Belize. This letter must be signed by the manager, president or by a legal representative of the company.
   iii) Certification by a Certified Public Accountant independent of the company:
      • Starting the date the company was established
      • Verifying the authenticity of the above mentioned letter
      • Certifying that the obligation signed in favor of the beneficiary is of no less than US $2,000.00 per month
   iv) The applicant must present two (2) bank references from the company that is sending the pension.
   v)   The company granting the pension must present a document outlining its pension scheme. Requirement ii) iii) iv) could be omitted where the company sending the pension is considered to be a Fortune Five Hundred Company.

3. <u>Background Check</u> - All applications are subject to a background check to be carried out by the Ministry of National Security.

Residency

All privileges, exemptions and regulations herein included are governed by the Retired Persons (Incentives) (Amendment) Act, 2001, and the ACT will serve as the basis for all purposes of interpretation.

1. Personal / Household Effects - Qualified Retired Persons under the program can qualify for duty and tax exemptions on new and used personal and household effects admitted as such by the Qualified Retirement Program Officer in charge of the program. A list of all items will corresponding values that will be imported must be submitted with the application. All items must be imported in country within 1 year after approval into the program.

2. Transportation -
   a. Motor Vehicle - Qualified Retired Persons are strongly encouraged to procure a vehicle in Belize. However, we will facilitate duty and tax exemption on an imported vehicle. Motor vehicles must be no older than 3 years from the present year.
   b. Light Aircraft - A Qualified Retired Person is entitled to import a light aircraft less than 17,000 kg. A Qualified Retired Person is required to have a valid Private Pilot license to fly in Belize. This license can be obtained by passing the requirements set by the Civil Aviation. However, if the participant has a valid pilot's license, that license only has to be validated by Civil Aviation Department in Belize.
   c. Boat - Any vessel that is used for personal purposes and for pleasure will be accepted under this program.

3. Disposal of Duty Free Items - If for whatever reason a Qualified Retired Person decides to sell, give away, lease or otherwise dispose of the approved means of transportation or personal effects to any person or entity within Belize, all duties and taxes must be paid by that person or entity to the proper authorities.

4. Offenses and Penalties - Any person who knowingly makes any false declaration or entry in order to qualify for or retain any exemption or privilege granted under the Retired Persons (Incentives) (Amendment) Act, 2001 commits an offence and shall be liable on summary conviction to a fine not exceeding five thousand dollars.

5. Fee Structure -
   a. A non-refundable application fee in the sum of $US 150.00 payable to the Belize Tourism Board must be submitted with the application.
   b. A program fee in the sum of US $1,000.00 payable to the Belize Tourism Board must be submitted upon acceptance into the program.
   c. Upon acceptance into the Program, a fee of US $2,000.00 must be paid to the Belize Tourism Board for the issuance of the Qualified Retired Person Residency Card.
   d. Each dependent is required to pay a Program Fee of US $750.00 to enter the Program.

Qualified Retired Persons Program

Residency Application*

- ✅ Statutory Due Diligence for Up to Two Persons
- ✅ Filing Residency Application
- ✅ Belize General 12.5% Sales Tax
- ✅ Government Application Fees *($150)*
- ✅ Government Program Fees *($1,000)*
- ✅ Government Card Fees *($200)*
- ✅ Application Time is 1 Business Day

Work Permit*

- ✅ Filing Work Permit Application
- ✅ Belize General 12.5% Sales Tax
- ✅ Government Application Fees *($1,125)*
- ✅ Government Expedite Fees *($900)*
- ✅ Application Time is 1 Business Day

* Legal Fees   Please contact our offices for specific details.

Commonwealth of Dominica

The Commonwealth of Dominica government established the acquisition of citizenship under Chapter VII, Section 101 of their Constitution. Section 8 of the 1978 Citizenship Act allowed for citizenship to be acquired upon meeting various requirements including the establishment of residency in Dominica. Later, under Section 20 of the amended Citizenship Act in 1991, such residency requirements were removed and Economic Citizenship was introduced to individuals and families of good character with the financial means to meet the government established cost. The current application process includes a mandatory interview which can be conducted in the Commonwealth of Dominica or another jurisdiction of choice. Although persons granted citizenship are ultimately published in the local "Official Gazette" as required by law, the Commonwealth of Dominica respects the privacy of applicants and no foreign government or authority is notified or informed that an application has been submitted or is under review. An English speaking country, Dominica is an attractive locality in which to obtain dual citizenship as passport holders maintain a positive international reputation with over 100 countries worldwide accepting Dominica nationals. Applications for dual citizenship in Dominica are processed and second passports are generally made available to approved applicants within 2-3 months.

Commonwealth of Dominica
Economic Citizenship

In Association With

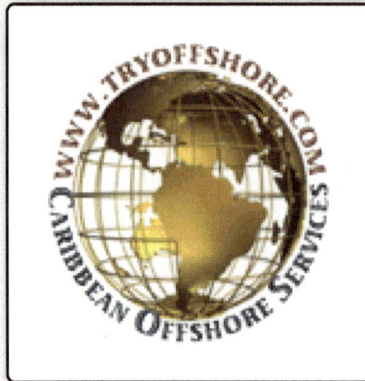

The Caribbean Offshore Services law firm is the official corporate service provider of APSI for all incorporation and dual citizenship services within the jurisdiction of Dominica.
APSI consulting services are inclusive within existing Caribbean Offshore Services fees.
There are absolutely no price increases whatsoever for our consulting services.

As the founder of **Caribbean Offshore Services**, attorney Alick Chambers Lawrence, S. C. is a Senior Counsel specializing in the areas of banking, litigation, legislative drafting, corporate law, offshore financial services, and intellectual property law, winning major cases for international companies. Prior to starting his private practice, Mr. Lawrence held many important positions in Dominica. Mr. Lawrence lives in Dominica with his wife and 4 children.

Alick C. Lawrence, S. C.

Attorney

1980	Dominica Island Scholar
1984	LLB (Upper Second Class Honors)
1986	Legal Education Certificate
1989	Certificate in Legislative Drafting

Experience

1986 – 1991 Government of Dominica
- State Attorney
- Acting Labour Commissioner
- Acting Registrar

1991 – Now Private Practice

Appointments

- Senior Counsel – (Equivalent of Queens Counsel in Canada or the UK)
- Chairman – National Development Foundation of Dominica Ltd.
- Chairman – Cardinal Airlines
- Chairman – Income Tax Appeal Board
- Chairman – Customs Appeal Tribunal
- Member – Constitution Review Commission
- Member – Working Committee on Offshore Sector Various Directorships

Legal Counsel to International Financial Institutions

- Dominica Agricultural Industrial and Development Bank
- Cable & Wireless Dominica Ltd.
- Dominica Unit Trust Corporation
- Dominica Export Import Agency
- Dominica Port Authority
- Citibank (Trinidad & Tobago)
- FirstCaribbean International bank
- National Development Corporation
- Dominica Water and Sewerage Company
- National Development Foundation of Dominica

Major Criminal and Civil Litigation in Dominica

- Represented the French construction company – Nord France Enterprise – in an arbitration against the local power company Dominica Electricity Services Ltd. Successful, the client was awarded approximately $12 million.
- Represented Cable & Wireless Dominica Ltd including the preparation of relevant documents and transactions leading to its acquisition of the Dominica assets of Cable and Wireless (West Indies) Ltd. valued at $120 million.

Letter of Good Standing

Commonwealth of Dominica

MINISTRY OF FINANCE
FINANCIAL SERVICES UNIT

Tel: (767) 266 3514 / 3558
Fax: (767) 448 0054
E-mail: fsu@cwdom.dm
Website: www.dominica.gov.dm

5ᵗʰ Floor, Financial Centre
Kennedy Avenue
Roseau
Commonwealth of Dominica

March 18, 2011

To Whom It May Concern:

This is to inform you that for many years now Mr. Alick C. Lawrence of Alick Lawrence Chambers has been actively promoting the Commonwealth of Dominica Offshore Sector which includes the Economic Citizenship Programme for the Government of the Commonwealth of Dominica.

Mr. Lawrence is our leading promoter and is in good standing with the Government of Dominica.

Additionally, Mr. Lawrence is a very prominent lawyer in Dominica

Yours truly,

SANDRA LLOYD-SAMUEL
(for) **DIRECTOR**
FINANCIAL SERVICES UNIT

"Professional & Productivity...Requisite for the Journey to Excellence"

Foreword

ALICK LAWRENCE CHAMBERS
ATTORNEYS-AT-LAW, NOTARIES PUBLIC

ALICK C.LAWRENCE, S.C., LL.B (HONS.), L.E.C.
ROSE-ANNE CHARLES, LL.B (HONS.), L.E.C., LL.M

June 7, 2013

Mr. Jay Butler
Via Soldini, 14
Chiasso
Ticino
6830 SWITZERLAND (CH)

Dear Mr. Butler,

Congratulations on your imminent publication, particularly the treatment given to the Economic Citizenship programme of the Commonwealth of Dominica. We are sure that your readers will find it very useful.

We take this opportunity to commend you for the work that you are doing in the field of economic citizenship. This is an area which has become of the utmost importance particularly in the last five years. The financial and legal expertise that you bring to the subject and the easy style of your writing makes your publication mandatory reading for anyone with interest in that field.

We are happy to be associated with such effort.

Best Regards,

ALICK LAWRENCE, S.C.

Nancy Whiticker House, 7 Old Street, Roseau, Dominica
Telephone: (767) 448-7697, Fax: (767) 448-3511
Email: lawrencea@cwdom.dm

Rodney Street, Portsmouth, Dominica, W.I.
Telephone:(767) 445-4373
Webpage:http://www.delphis.dm/alick/lawrence.htm

About the Commonwealth of Dominica

Activities

'Majestic' may best describe the lush green forest covered mountains of the Commonwealth of Dominica. Nature enthusiasts can revel in a myriad of activities including canyoning, exotic bird watching, hiking, jeep safari tours, natural hot springs and pools, river kayaking and tubing, scuba diving, sea turtle watching, snorkeling, sport fishing, waterfalls, whale watching, and more. Ports in the two urban cities of Roseau and Portsmouth support large cruise ships to dock bringing passengers who enjoy fine dining, dancing, shopping, exploring and relaxing.

Climate

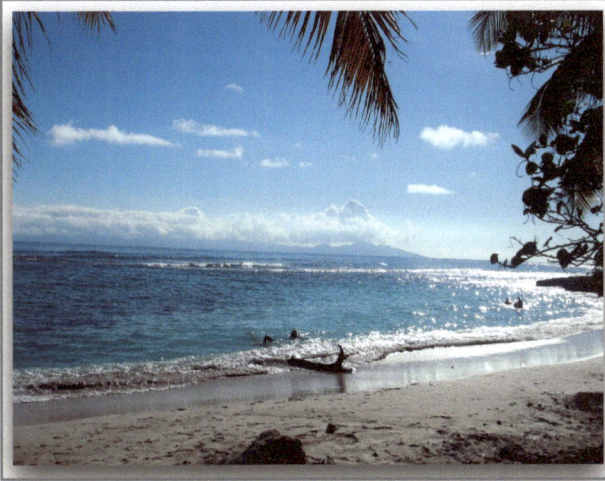

Dominica has a wet tropical climate moderated by Northeastern trade winds. The island experiences rainfall throughout the year with its heaviest rains arriving in June and lessening in October. Median temperatures vary less than 3°C throughout the island with average temperatures of 26°C in the winter to 32°C in the summer. Dominica is fortunate in that it has an ample supply of fresh water brought in from the Northeastern trade winds. The leeward west coast receives a moderate 180 cm of rain annually while windward east coast accumulations exceed 500 cm. The exposed eastward facing mountainsides receive up to 900 cm of rain annually, which ranks as the highest accumulation of annual rainfall anywhere on the planet. Humidity correlates to rainfall patterns and recorded to be as high as 90% in the capital city of Roseau. Dominica is located in a hurricane region and is often subject to intense wind and rain from hurricanes.

Culture

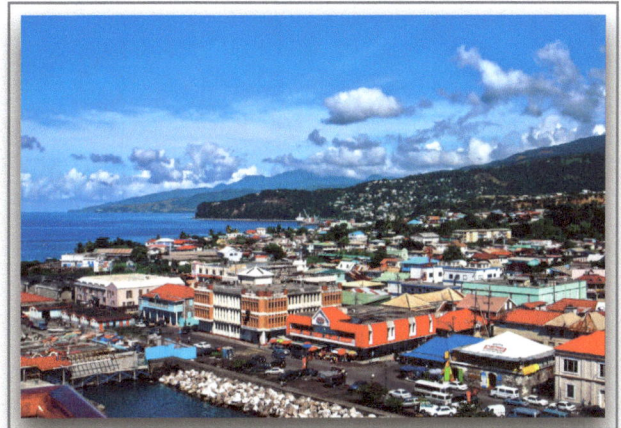

Indigenous Dominicans are 'Caribs' and live on an 15 square kilometer establishment for the preservation of their identity. Over 90% of the general population in Dominica have historical roots dating back to slaves brought to the island in the 17th and 18th century. Eighty percent of Dominicans considers themselves to be Roman Catholic with conservative values. Annual festivals include a three day Catholic Carnival celebrated prior to Ash Wednesday, the Carnival Queen Pageant, and the World Creole Music Festival. Traditional staple Dominican diets includes fresh local chicken, goat, lamb or beef covered in a spicy pepper sauce of fruit concoction. Rich terrain lends to a variety fruits from tamarind to passion fruit. Hibiscus and medicinal teas originate in Dominica.

Economy and Offshore Financial Services

Bananas are the principle agricultural crop in the Commonwealth of Dominica. Banana production employs in excess of one-third of the entire nation's work force. Given the vulnerability of weather conditions and external commodity prices, Dominica has strived to diversify its agricultural production into coffee, patchouli, aloe vera, mangoes, guavas, and papayas as well as to improve its tourism and offshore financial services industries. The Commonwealth of Dominica has high, rugged mountains and, being mostly volcanic, possesses few beaches in comparison to neighboring countries. However the freshwater hot springs, waterfalls and rain-forests make the spas in Dominica an attractive destination, plus the ability for deepwater cruise ships to reach port have given rise to eco-tourism. The Commonwealth of Dominica is a member of the Organization of Eastern Caribbean States (OECS), the Eastern Caribbean Currency Union (ECCU), and the fifteen member strong Caribbean Community (CARICOM). Asset Protection Services of America offers complete economic citizenship in the Commonwealth of Dominica.

Geography

The Commonwealth of Dominica is located in the Caribbean Sea halfway between the island of Guadeloupe (48 km to the north) and the island of Martinique (40 km to the south). For centuries sailing ships crossing the Atlantic ocean would take advantage of strong prevailing trade winds which, at the end of their voyage from Europe or Africa, inexorably led them to one of four specific 'windward' islands. The windward islands consist of the Commonwealth of Dominica, Saint Lucia, Grenada, and Saint Vincent and the Grenadines. The Commonwealth of Dominica, often referred to as Dominica, is known for its rugged terrain, heavy rains, and lush flora and fauna. The highest elevation on the island is Morne Diablotins standing at 1,447 meters above sea level. Runoff from the rain-drenched lands form spectacular pools, cascading waterfalls and support a wide array of wildlife.

History

Although the Arawaks are credited among the first inhabitants of Dominica, Carib tribes overthrew them and settled in during the 14th century. The Caribs called the island Waitikubuli which means "tall is her body". When Christopher Columbus first spotted the island, he named it "Domenica" after the day of the week in which he located it. The Spanish were unable to settle on the island as they were met with fierce resistance from the Caribs. Even the French and English agreed that the islands of Dominica and St Vincent should remain untouched territories and left entirely to the Caribs due to their ferocious fighting abilities. And so the islands remained neutral for more than a century until the need to pillage the natural resources of Dominica drove the French and English to fight for possession of Dominica. In 1761 the British overtook Dominica and officially held the territory from 1763-1978. After the slave abolition act of 1834, Dominica became the only Caribbean island to have black-controlled legislature in the 19th century. The Crown of England ensured the legislative powers of the black population diminished over time until such erosion re-established a crown colony in 1896. For nearly a hundred years Dominicans struggled to have the voice of the people reach the ears of their governing rulers. In modern day, despite several devastating hurricanes and fluctuations in banana prices, Dominica has as stable a government as any other country in the Caribbean.

Interesting Facts

Capital	**Population**
Roseau	71,293
Official Language	**GDP**
English	$977 Million
Government	**Currency**
Unitary Parliamentary Republic	East Caribbean Dollar
Laws	**Driving**
Common Law	Left
Independence Day	**Internet**
November 3rd, 1978	.dm
Total Area	**Calling Code**
750 Km2	+1 (767)

Constitution of the Commonwealth of Dominica

Chapter VII of the Commonwealth of Dominica Constitution allows Parliament to pass laws to grant citizenship to persons who are not entitled under preceding sections:

Section 101. There shall be such provisions as may be made by Parliament for -
- **(a)** the acquisition of citizenship of Dominica by persons who are not eligible or who are no longer eligible to become citizens of Dominica under the provisions of this Chapter:
- **(b)** depriving of his citizenship of Dominica any person who is a citizen of Dominica otherwise than by virtue of section 97, 98 or 99 of this Constitution;
- **(c)** the renunciation by any person of his citizenship of Dominica.

1978 Citizenship Act (Amended 1991)

In 1991, the Citizenship Act was amended waiving all former residency requirements from the original 1978 Act, which officially introduced the concept of a Economic Citizenship.

Section 20. (1) The Minister may by Regulations make provision generally for the carrying out of this Act or of Chapter VII of the Constitution and in particular for-
- **(a)** prescribing anything which is to be prescribed in relation to or in connection with citizenship;
- **(b)** the registration of any thing required or authorized to be registered;
- **(c)** the administration and taking of oaths of allegiance, for the time within which such oaths shall be taken and for the registration of such oaths;
- **(d)** the giving of any notice required or authorized to be given to or by any person under this Act;
- **(e)** the cancellation of the registration of and the cancellation and amendment of certificates of naturalization relating to persons deprived of citizenship under this Act and for requiring such certificates to be delivered up for those purposes;
- **(f)** the registration by consular officers or other officers in the service of Dominica of the births and deaths of persons of any class or description born or dying in a foreign State;
- **(g)** enabling the births and deaths of citizens of Dominica in countries in which Dominica has no diplomatic or consular representatives to be registered by persons serving in the consular, diplomatic or foreign service of any other country, or by a person authorized in that behalf by the Minister;
- **(h)** the imposition and recovery of fees in respect of any application made to the Minister in respect of any registration, or the making of any declaration or the grant of any certificate, or the taking of any oath of allegiance, authorized to be made, granted or taken under this Act, and in respect of supplying a certified copy of any notice, certificate, order, declaration or entry given, granted or made as aforesaid; and for the application of such fees.

Documentation

The following is a list of required documentation to submit an Application for Economic Citizenship in the Commonwealth of Dominica.

1.) A letter of interest in applying for citizenship addressed to the Prime Minister.
2.) Two (2) completed and notarized Application Forms for each person (Form 12 Provided)
3.) Certified color-copy of Passport
4.) Certified color-copy of Birth Certificate (Applicable for all family members)
5.) Marriage Certificate or Dissolution of Marriage where applicable
6.) Police Record with fingerprints from country of birth and country of residence (if different) for each applicant sixteen (16) years of age and older
7.) One (1) professional reference letter
8.) Two (2) personal reference letters
9.) One (1) bank reference letter
10.) Letter of employment. Business owners shall provide an audited financial statement
11.) Letter of recommendation from the head of the school/university for children between 16 and 18 years of age
12.) Detailed Business Background Reports / Resume / Curriculum Vitae
13.) Most recent Income Tax Return
14.) Notarized copies of University / College Diplomas
15.) Eight (8) passport size photos for each applicant
16.) Declaration of source of funds
17.) Statutory Declaration
18.) Medical Report (Form Provided)
19.) Notarized Disclosure Form (Provided)

Language Requirements

Although the official language in the Commonwealth of Dominica is English, if the applicant(s) do not speak any English, they may still proceed with the application process so long as the application supplies a competent translator for the due diligence interviews and meeting with the Prime Minister, etc. Additionally, all documentation would need to be duly translated into english and certified.

Passport Duration

Dominica passports are valid for a 10 year duration and 5 years for children under 16 years of age. Passports which need to be renewed as a result of being expired, or for a lack of additional space for visa stamps cost only $60 (USD), and passports which need to be replaced as a result of being lost, damaged or stolen cost $190 (USD).

Procedural Steps

Step 1

All professional legal fees shall be paid in full. Asset Protection Services, in conjunction with our legal provider located in the Commonwealth of Dominica, will lead you through obtaining and completing the required paperwork for the due diligence agency.

The necessary Disclosure Form shall be provided to print-out and e-mail back to us. Based on the information and data submitted, we will advise you on the paperwork needed to move forward in your application process and ask you to make corrections where necessary.

Step 2

We will contact an investigating agency, on your behalf, which is authorized by the Government of Dominica to conduct the due diligence interview and background check for you and any accompanying applicants. The investigating agency (such as Bishops Investigative Services Worldwide) will provide a quote for their services based on your particular case. The fees for the investigation shall be paid by the applicant directly to the account of the investigative agency.

When all of the original documents and fees are received by the said agency, the investigation shall commence at an agreed upon time and location. Experience indicates that it takes about 45-60 days to receive the due diligence results from the investigating agency.

Step 3

Upon receipt of the due diligence results, the Government will send a letter of comfort regarding the acceptability of the application which also serves as a letter of invitation to visit Dominica for the final interview.

You shall then be required to transfer the prescribed investment directly into an account of the Dominican government. Payment for the application of Dominican citizenship and second passports requires 100% prepayment.

The primary family applicant / investor should come for the interview with a special committee headed by the Attorney General, a senior policy officer and member of the Financial Services Unit. Such interviews are held every second and last Friday of the month. It is possible to arrive the afternoon prior to your scheduled final interview, or earlier if you wish to familiarize yourself with the country and its people. We shall provide you with possible interview questions and answers to help prepare you for your interview.

Upon arrival, you will be met at the airport by our representative and we will do everything reasonably possible to ensure your stay in Dominica is enjoyable. It is a standard procedure to wait from 10 to 30 days after the interview for your Certificate of Naturalization and Passport. It is not necessary to wait for it in Dominica, unless you wish to extend your holiday in the country. As soon as we receive the documents from the Commonwealth of Dominica authorities, they will be sent to you by express courier post.

Taxes

The Commonwealth of Dominica has no capital gains tax, no inheritance tax, and any income derived from outside Dominica is not subject to any income tax.

Visa-Free Entry

In addition to the 26 Schengen member states requiring pre-approval, herein is a list of 76 countries which allow visa-free (or stamped on arrival*) access to Dominica passport holders.

Anguilla	Guernsey	Peru
Antigua & Barbuda	Guyana	Philippines
Aruba	Haiti	Pitcairn
Bahamas	Hong Kong	Rwanda*
Barbados	Iran*	Samoa*
Belarus*	Iraq*	Sao Tome & Principe*
Belize	Ireland	Sark
Bermuda	Isle of Man	Seychelles*
Bhutan*	Isles des Saintes	Singapore
Bonaire	Israel	Salomon Islands*
British Virgin Islands	Jamaica	St Barthélemy
Brunei	Jersey	St Helena
Burundi*	Jordan*	St Kitts & Nevis
Cambodia*	Kenya*	St Lucia
Cape Verde Islands*	Korea	St Maarten
Cayman Islands	Kuwait*	St Vincent & the Grenadines
China*	Lao Peoples Dem. Rep.*	Suriname
Chile*	Lesotho	Syria*
Colombia	Macao	Tanzania
Comoros Islands*	Madagascar*	Thailand*
Cook Islands	Marshall Islands*	Timor-Liste*
Costa Rica	Malaysia	Togo*
Cuba	Maldives*	Tonga*
Curacao	Marie Galante	Trinidad & Tobago
Djibouti*	Martinique	Turks & Caicos
Dominican Republic*	Mauritius	Turkey*
East Timor*	Micronesia	Tuvalu
Egypt*	Montserrat	Uganda*
Ethiopia*	Mozambique*	United Arab Emirates*
El Salvador	Namibia	United Kingdom
Fiji	Nepal*	Vanuatu
Gambia*	Nicaragua	Venezuela
Georgia*	Niue	Zambia
Gibraltar	Northern Mariana Islands*	Zimbabwe
Grenada	Palau Islands*	
Guadeloupe	Panama	

Economic Citizenship
Current as of September 1st, 2012

Package A	**Single Applicant Contribution** *(Per individual Applicant 18 years of age or older)*	**$100,000***
Package B	**Family Application One Contribution** *(Applicant 18 years of age or older plus one Spouse)*	**$175,000***
Package C	**Family Application Two Contribution** *(Applicant plus one Spouse and up to two Children under 18)*	**$200,000***
Package D	**Family Application Two Contribution** *(Applicant plus one Spouse and two Children under 18 years of age, plus $50,000 for each additional person 18 years of age or under)*	**$200,000 + $50,000***

Gov. Fees		
	Government Application Fee	**$1,000 per Application**
	Government Naturalization Fee	**$550 per Person**
	Government Processing Fee	**$200 per Person**
	Government Stamp Fee	**$15 per Application**
	Government Due Diligence Fee	***See Below***

The Government of Dominica appoints a due diligence investigating agency to perform all background investigations and, as the fees are paid directly to such investigating agency, they are beyond our control. Given the disparity in the number and ages of family members, countries of current citizenship, permanent residency or domicile, prices may range anywhere from $3,000 to $10,000 per person. If an applicant wishes for the interview to be held 'overseas' there is a fee of $3,000 and the applicant must absorb the expense of the interview committee of three (3) persons going to the interview including the expense of air fare, hotel and a per diem allowance.

* Legal Fees   Please contact our offices for specific details.

Dominican Republic

The Dominican Republic is one of the least expensive jurisdictions in the world in which to obtain Citizenship. Regulations accepting new applicants are easily met upon good, drug-free health and a clean police record. The Dominican Republic is a founding member of the United Nations enjoying unrestricted trade relationships with the United States, the European Union and most, if not all, of Africa and Asia. Applicants are required to travel to the nearest Dominican Republic Consulate and, upon contingent approval, visit the city of Santo Domingo in the Dominican Republic to submit their legal documentation and take a mandatory government medical test. After completing this initial process applicants shall wait 6 months and, upon provisional approval, may proceed for citizenship by investment, naturalization, rentista or retiree. Household items may then be imported duty-free and residents may begin living and working in the Dominican Republic. The government does not require physical residency in the Dominican Republic during the remainder of the application process nor after Citizenship is granted. Whether you wish to live and work in the Dominican Republic or would enjoy traveling to the Caribbean a few times to obtain dual Citizenship, the Dominican Republic is an attractive and inexpensive country in which to obtain a second passport.

Dominican Republic
Economic Citizenship

In Association With

The Guzmàn Ariza law firm is the official corporate service provider of APSI for all incorporation and dual citizenship services within the jurisdiction of the Dominican Republic. APSI consulting services are inclusive within existing Guzmàn Ariza fees. There are absolutely no price increases whatsoever for our consulting services.

Guzmán Ariza is a national law and business consulting firm – the first and only one in the Dominican Republic. Founded in 1927, their eight offices are strategically located to serve you in every major business and tourism center in the Dominican Republic. Their multilingual attorneys and business consultants are equipped to help you across a wide variety of practice areas. Guzmàn Ariza is a State Capital Global Law Firm Group Member Firm (with 140 top law firms comprised of over 11,500 attorneys in 80 countries worldwide). The lawyers at Guzmàn Ariza have served as experts on the laws of the Dominican Republic in foreign jurisdictions.

Attorney

D. Antonio Guzmàn L.

(1906-2001)

Our firm was founded by Lic. D. Antonio Guzmán L. in 1927, after graduating that same year from the University of Santo Domingo Law School. Mr. Guzmán soon became one of the most accomplished practitioners in the Dominican Republic in the areas of Civil Litigation and Estates Law although his practice was wide ranging as was common at the time. In 1962, Mr. Guzmán was the lead counsel for the prosecution in the most celebrated trial of the last century in the Dominican Republic: the trial of the murderers of the Mirabal sisters, the national heroes killed for their opposition to the Trujillo dictatorship. His private practice as an attorney encompassed more than eight decades, from 1927 until 2000. In the public arena, he was a member of the Constitutional Assembly which adopted a new Constitution in 1941, President of the City Council of San Francisco de Macorís (1961-1962) and member of the National Development Council (1968-1974). In 1977, he was presented for his achievements in the law with the "Order of Duarte, Sánchez y Mella, Gran Cruz Placa de Plata", the highest award granted by the Dominican government to a private citizen. In 1983, Universidad Católica Nordestana received him as "Doctor Honoris Causa.". A book about Mr. Guzmán's life, *Memoirs of a Small Town Lawyer*, was published in 2007.

Foreword

GUZMÁN ARIZA
ABOGADOS y CONSULTORES

www.drlawyer.com • info@drlawyer.com

Santo Domingo
San Francisco de Macorís
Sosúa
Cabrera
Las Terrenas
Samaná
Bávaro (Punta Cana)
La Romana

Miembro exclusivo en la
República Dominicana de

SCG LEGAL
A Worldwide Network of Leading Law Firms

July 31, 2013

Mr. Jay Butler
Via Soldini 14
Chiasso, Ticino
6830 Switzerland (CH)

Re: Collaborative Agreement for Immigration Services in the Dominican Republic

Dear Mr. Butler,

It has been a pleasure for us at Guzman Ariza to have established a collaborative agreement with you since December 1st, 2011, to offer Immigration Services in the Dominican Republic through your company, Asset Protection Services International and Corporate Service Provider.

We embrace this opportunity to express our gratitude and commend you for the publication of your book on Economic Citizenship. We believe it is highly informative and exquisitely prepared. We hope to continue the working relationship we have developed with you so far and we congratulate you in advance for the success that we foresee you will accomplish with this book.

We sincerely thank you for the trust you have expressed in our law firm.

Very truly yours,

GUZMAN ARIZA Attorneys at Law

Fabio J. Guzmán Saladín, Esq., MBA

Guzmán Ariza (Santo Domingo), S.R.L. • RNC 1-30-36274-2 • Tel.: (809) 255-0980 • Fax: (809) 255-0940
Calle Ernesto de la Maza No. 35, Mirador Norte, Santo Domingo, República Dominicana

About the Dominican Republic

Activities

The Dominican Republic offers a wide variety of outdoor activities including canyoning, canoeing, catamaran cruises, caving and cave diving, deep-sea fishing, world-class golfing, helicopter rides, hiking, horseback riding, kiteboarding, mountain biking, "Ocean World" tours, paragliding, quad-riding, rafting, sailing, scenic small engine plane flights, scuba-diving, snorkeling, surfing, wake boarding, whale watching, windsurfing and more.

Climate

With temperatures averaging 25°C year-round, the Dominican Republic enjoys a tropical 28°C near sea level and 18°C at higher elevations. The mountains rarely, if ever, go below 0°C and protected plains infrequently exceed 40°C. The northern portion of the country will experience pleasant brief afternoon showers from November through January, with the coolest months being in January and February, while the southern portion of the country is more inclined to receive its periodic rainfall from May through November. The driest part of the country is located in the west, but nationwide annual rainfall still reaches around 150 centimeters on average. The hottest month is August, with the most delightful times of the year considered to be in the spring.

Culture

The Dominican Republic population is represented by diverse nationalities and, in addition to Spanish as the official language, English, French, German and Italian are commonly spoken. The culture was predominately influence by Spain and such Spanish heritage is expressed in the people's passion for music, dance and art. There are national theaters, dance troupes, open-air art galleries and outdoor festivals throughout the country. Roman Catholicism is the primary religious denomination with one Archdiocese, over 500 clergy and the cathedral of "Santa Maria La Menor" dating back to 1540. The Dominican Republic is home to some of the world's most modern villas, resorts and hotels, elegant restaurants, exquisite shopping and professional golf courses.

Economy and Offshore Financial Services

The Dominican Republic economy is driven in large part by the services sector such as tourism and light manufacturing. The United States, Canada and the European Union are the largest countries to whom the Dominican Republic exports goods, while Venezuela, Mexico and the United States are the three largest countries with whom the Dominican Republic imports goods. Principle exports include clothing, cigars, sugar, coffee, tobacco, fruits, vegetables, flowers, tropical plants, cocoa, and gold and silver. Principal imports include petroleum, industrial and agricultural raw materials, capital goods, wood, pharmaceuticals and food products. Asset Protection Services of America offers complete citizenship and passport services in the Dominican Republic.

Geography

The Dominican Republic and Haiti are on the island of *Hispaniola* and are the only two countries in the Caribbean to share the same island. The Cordillera Central mountain range is one of 5 mountain ranges running through the Dominican Republic. "Pico Duarte" is the highest point in the Dominican Republic and in the Caribbean reaching a respectable 3,087 meters above sea level. With 1,633 kilometers of coastline, the Dominican Republic possess spectacular cliffs, long stretches of white sandy beaches and crystal clear turquoise water. The "Playa Grande" beach has been voted among the top 10 beaches in the world. The Dominican Republic landscape contains fresh water lagoons, ocean coves, coral reefs, small islands, cays, inlets, national parks, rivers, lakes and waterfalls. There is a diverse terrain with semi-desert plains to lush valleys and tropical rain forests with a total of 27 different climatic zones.

History

Christopher Columbus was greeted by the Taino (meaning "good" or "Knoble") Indians upon his initial visit to the Dominican Republic in the late 14th century. The first European settlements were built on the northern part of the island, where Puerto Plata is now, and exploited the natural resources such as gold from the Cibao Valley. The city of Santo Domingo was established in 1496 and governed by Christopher Columbus's brother Bartholomew. Many within the Taino native population valiantly resist Spanish occupation and were brutally tortured or murdered for uprising against such tyranny. The populous however, lacked the bodily immunities to protect themselves against diseases like small pox and was eventually reduced to fewer than 50,000 people within 25 years. Once Spain had removed a vast majority of the areas natural resources, they turned their interests to Mexico and the territory was controlled by the French into the 18th century. Local resistance to the French and Spanish enslavement of people lasted for decades and after a military struggle with Haiti, the Repùblica Dominicana was finally declared on February 27th, 1844. The Dominican Republic was subject to a multitude of military leaders and corrupt political rulers for well over a century. It wasn't until the eight year "intervention" by America that civil uprisings were quelled and the country's legal system was restructured.

Capital Santo Domingo	**Population** 9,378,818
Official Language Spanish	**GDP** $93 Billion
Government Democratic Republic	**Currency** Dominican Peso
Laws Common Law	**Driving** Right
Independence Day August 16th, 1865	**Internet** .do
Total Area 48,442 Km2	**Calling Code** +1 (809)

Interesting Facts

Notices

Immigration Laws

Beginning June 1st of 2012, residency status in the Dominican Republic is governed by Immigration Law No. 285-04 and Immigrations Regulation No. 631-11.

Constitution of the Dominican Republic

The newly reformed Constitution of the Dominican Republic received Congressional approval in October of 2009 and was enacted on January 26th, 2010. Below are the most important articles as they pertain to citizenship.

Article 18 established the following as a Dominican national:
- **a.)** A person born to a mother or father with Dominican nationality, regardless of the country in which the parent lives;
- **b.)** A person born in the Dominican;
- **c.)** A person marrying a Dominican national;
- **d.)** The direct descendants of Dominicans residing in a foreign country.
- **e.)** *A person who is naturalized as a Dominican national. (Emphasis added)*

Article 19 stipulates that a naturalized citizen is not eligible to hold the office of President or Vice-President of any branch with the Dominican Republic government, and is not required to take up arms against his or her country of origin.

Article 20 permits dual nationalities, and a Dominican may acquire a foreign nationality without the risk of losing Dominican nationality.

Article 21 bestows the rights of citizenship upon a Dominican national only to persons who have reached the age of eighteen years of age. Minors can be a Dominican national, but will not have citizenship rights nor a National ID card for Citizens (*Cedulà de Identidad Personal*) unless they are married or until they reach the age of 18.

Article 22 entitles citizens the right to vote, run for public office, vote on referendums, make requests of public interest to policy makers, and report public official's misconduct in the performance of their duties.

Article 23 permits citizenship to be revoked for conviction of assisting or participating in deliberate attacks or harm against the interests of the Dominican Republic, including treason, espionage, conspiracy, or taking up arms against the Dominican Republic.

Article 24 permits citizenship to be suspended for the duration of (i) a sentence for a felony conviction, (ii) a legally declared incompetency, (iii) acceptance to a position with a foreign State within the Dominican Republic not preauthorized by the Executive Branch, and (d) a violation of any of the conditions of naturalization.

Article 25 grants foreign nationals the same rights and duties as natural born Dominican nationals, with one exception. Foreign nationals may not participate in political activities in the foreign national's country of origin except to vote in elections.

Article 221 ensures local and foreign investments are treated equally under the law, with only a few restrictions under Constitutional and Statutory law.

Household Goods

Household goods are considered belongings which would commonly be found in the home such as televisions, personal computers, furniture, kitchenware, clothing, artwork, etc. A personal vehicle is also considered a household good and shall be considered duty free if ownership can be demonstrated for at least one year, while the age of the vehicle cannot exceed five (5) years. Boats are not considered a household good and shall be subject import duties or tax.

Insurances Waiver

Law No. 285-04 mandates that residency applicants must obtain local insurance to cover medical and repatriation expenses. However such requirement have *temporarily* been waived by the Immigrations Department and may be subject to reinstatement at anytime without notice.

FATCA

The Dominican Republic Tax Authorities have subscribed an agreement with the United States Internal Revenue Service (IRS) and from January 1st, 2014 shall exchange information in accordance with the Foreign Account Tax Compliance Act (FACTA).

All Dominican Republic banks, receiving monies from U.S. citizens above the cumulative sum of US$50,000 in a calendar year will be obliged to retain 30% of such monies in accordance with the execution of provisions within the FACTA legislation. Such withholdings shall also apply to any Dominican Republic corporation or entity in which a U.S. citizen holds more than 10% of the shares in such company. For more information, see Issue N° 8 of our monthly newsletter "Cover Your Assets" dedicated to helping decipher such new FATCA laws.
(http://assetprotectionservices.com/apsi/resources/cover-your-assets.html)

Firearms

Firearms may be permitted in the country if the interested party obtains a permit. The requirements for obtaining a permit are:
- Certification by competent authorities stating the firearm (serial) is clean
- Drug Test
- Firing Range Test
- Government Taxes
- Psychiatric Test

Pets

Household animals (such as dogs and cats for example) are not considered household goods and shall be subject to government tax. However, such animals may be permitted into the country if the owner can provide documentation less than thirty (30) days old from a veterinarian that all of the animals are current with their shots and have a clean bill of health.

Prohibited

Foreign nationals are prohibited by state from entering the Dominican Republic for residency purposes in the following cases:
1. Contagious illness threatens public health, except, under certain requirements, when sponsored by relatives living in the Dominican Republic;
2. Mental illness or physical disabilities, with certain exceptions;
3. Conviction of a crime (drugs, human trafficking, prostitution, terrorism, and other offenses);
4. Previous deportation without re-entry permit of prohibition from entry the country;

Taxes

Dominican Republic taxation is primarily territorial. All income derived from work or business activities within the DR is taxable, whereas all income derived from work or business activities outside the DR is not taxable. The exception to the principle of territoriality is income from financial sources abroad. A Dominican (or foreign resident) receiving income from financial investments (such as stocks, bonds, certificates of deposits, etc) must pay taxes in the Dominican Republic on their income from those investments. Pensions and Social Security benefits are exempt. For Resident Foreigners, this obligation only begins three (3) years after obtaining residency (Article 271).

The Dominican Republic has a sliding individual income tax rate based on the AGI (Adjusted Gross Income) scale as seen below in Dominican Republic Peso (DOP).

Income up to $371,124.00	Exempt
Income from $371,124.01 up to $556,685.00	15% of the Surplus of $371,124.01
Income from $556,685.01 up to $773,173.00	$27,834.00 plus 20% of the surplus of $556,685.01
Income from $773,173.01 or more	$71,132.00 plus 25% of the surplus of $773,124.01

Although a Dominican Republic national may be a citizen of the Dominican Republic, they are not a resident for tax purposes if not physically present in the Dominican Republic for more than 182 days in any given year.

Dominican nationals are only obligated to pay taxes on income received from their worldwide financial investments (such as stocks, bonds, mutual funds and CD'S, etc) if they are residing in the Dominican Republic for more than 182 days in a given year.

The Dominican Republic has a flat 29% corporate income tax on company profits (after allowable deductions).

Visa-Free Entry

This is a list of 40 countries and territories which allow visa-free access to holders of a Dominican Republic Passport.

Argentina
Armenia
Bermuda
Cape Verde Islands
Chile
Colombia
Commonwealth of Dominica
Comoros Islands
Cook Islands
Cuba
Ecuador
East Timor
Georgia
Hong Kong
Israel
Japan
South Korea
Macao
Madagascar
Malaysia

Marshall Islands
Micronesia
Montserrat
Mozambique
Nicaragua
Niue
Palau Islands
Peru
Philippines
Samoa
Seychelles
Singapore
Solomon Islands
St Lucia
St Vincent and the Grenadines
Tanzania
Tunisia
Uganda
Uruguay
Venezuela

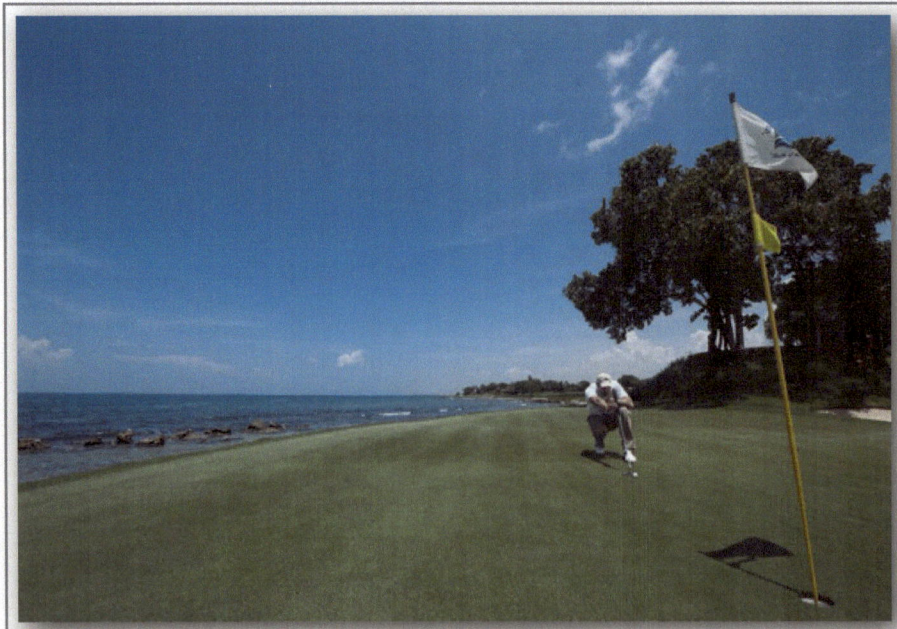

Citizenship with Passport

Foreign nationals seeking residency in the Dominican Republic fall into two categories:
1.) those who first must apply first for temporary residency; and
2.) those who may apply immediately for permanent residency.

Flow-Chart

	Dominican Republic Consulate	Dominican Republic LLC	Provisional Residency	Provisional Residency Renewal	Permanent Residency	Permanent Residency Renewal	Citizenship & Passport
Investor Residency	X	X			X		X
Naturalization	X		X	X X X X	X	X	X
Rentista Residency	X				X	X	X
Retiree Residency	X				X	X	X

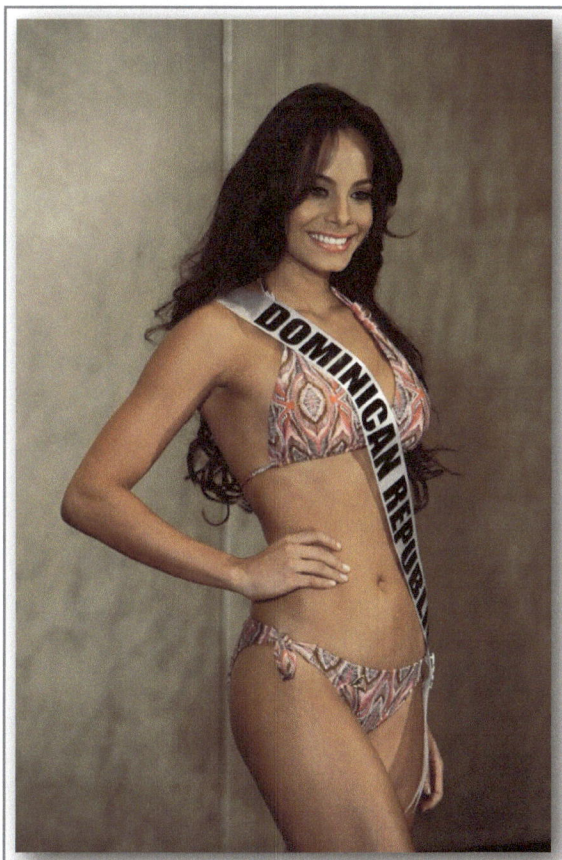

Total Estimated Cost and Time
Prices do not include travel related expenses.

Investor	$13,927	1 to 1.5 Years
Naturalization	$13,462	6.5 to 7 Years
Rentista	$ 6,128	1.5 to 2 Years
Retiree	$ 6,128	1.5 to 2 Years

Naturalization

(D.R. Consulate --> Provisional Residency --> Four (4) Provisional Residency Renewals
--> Permanent Residency --> Permanent Residency Renewal --> Citizenship)

Beginning June 1st of 2012, Dominican Republic Naturalization Applicants who have initiated their Naturalization protection (without having yet obtained their Permanent Residency) are required to renew their Provisional Residency for four (4) consecutive years, and then apply for (and renew) their Permanent Residency prior to submitting the final application for citizenship.

Investor Residency

(D.R. Consulate --> Formation of a Dominican Republic Limited Liability Company
--> Permanent Residency --> Citizenship)

1. Upon successful completion and the two-year Permanent Residency and the Permanent Residency Renewal, Applicants may then apply for the Investor Residency.

2. Applicants must provide a proof of funds in the form of a "Certificate of Investment" issued by the Department of Export and Investments (CEI-RD).

3. Applicants shall invest invest at least $200,000 (USD) or more into the Dominican Republic in the form of a commercial real estate estate investment, local business (including free zones and government contracts), local financial instruments or any other comparable investment which "furthers the overall economic advancement of the Dominican Republic" as approved by the General Immigrations Board.

4. Applicants shall form a Dominican Republic Limited Liability Company:
   ‣ Pay a 1% Valuation Tax on the assets held by the entity
   ‣ Pay 29% Corporate Income Tax on any earnings of the entity, less allowable deductions
   ‣ File an annual Corporate Income Tax Return until the entity is Properly Dissolved

Rentista Residency
(D.R. Consulate --> Permanent Residency --> Permanent Residency Renewal --> Citizenship)

1. Upon successful completion and the two-year Permanent Residency and the Permanent Residency Renewal, Applicants may then apply for the Rentista Residency program:

2. Applicants shall provide documentation of receiving a minimum monthly income in the amount of $2,000 (USD) for a period of no less than five (5) years. Such Documents may include any combination of the following
    ‣ Certified Financial Instrument (Stocks, Bonds, Mutual Funds, Investments, etc)
    ‣ Rental Agreement
    ‣ Investment in a Company
    ‣ Any other Document issued by a Third Party which states the Applicant receives no less than $2,000 in passive monthly income (Later to be deposited into a D.R. bank account)
    ‣ Married Couples shall qualify with $2,250 (USD) of the aforementioned income
    ‣ Such Documentation must be Authenticated by a Dominican Republic Consulate

Retiree Residency
(D.R. Consulate --> Permanent Residency --> Permanent Residency Renewal --> Citizenship)

1. Upon successful completion and the two-year Permanent Residency and the Permanent Residency Renewal, Applicants may then apply for the Retiree Residency program:

2. Applicants shall provide documentation of receiving a minimum monthly income in the amount of $1,500 USD (plus $250 USD per dependent) for a period of no less than five (5) consecutive years.
    ‣ Most any form of passive income is acceptable (Stocks, Bonds, Investments, etc)
    ‣ An Official Document from the Financial or Government Institution whereby the Applicant receives the passive income
    ‣ Such Documentation must beAuthenticated by a Dominican Republic Consulate

Dominican Republic Consulate
(Naturalization / Investor / Rentista / Retiree)

1. Applicants shall travel to the nearest Dominican Republic Consulate and apply for a residency visa. The cost for such a residency visa is US$90 (or €90 in the Euro Zone) and is valid for one entry lasting for an initial period of 60 days. It is no longer possible to apply for any residency visas from within the Dominican Republic. Requirements for the visa application are the following.

    Applicants shall present all the following documentation duly translated in Spanish and apostilled from the issuing country of birth or authenticated from a Dominican Consulate:

    ‣ **Original Birth Certificate**
    ‣ **Original Marriage License** (if applicable)
    ‣ **Certificate of No Criminal Record** (applicable for applicants 18 years of age or older) from the authorities in the country of birth (or if residing outside the country of birth for more than 5 years, from the country of residence)
    ‣ **Eight Passport Photos** (2" x 2") with 4 front and 4 right-hand side profiles. White background required and any accessories such as jewelry or sunglasses are prohibited
    ‣ **Copy of University Degree** (if applicable)
    ‣ **Original Passport** valid for at least a stay of 60 days in the Dominican Republic
    ‣ **Medical Certificate** from the health authorities of the country of domicile
    ‣ **Photocopy of National ID** from the current country of residence and, if the applicant resides in a third country, Photocopy of residency card in such country
    ‣ **Photocopy of Residency Card** (Applicable if the Applicant is residing in a 3rd country)
    ‣ **Notarized Letter of Guarantee** from a Dominican person or corporation (Guzmàn Ariza shall provide this letter
    ‣ **Affidavit of Solvency** of the guarantor backed by evidence of solvency such as bank deposits or property titles
    ‣ **Documents Justifying Visa** be granted, such as a work contract from a company within the Dominican Republic

2. If the residency visa is approved, the Consulate will stamp the residency visa on the Applicant's passport and the application file will be forwarded to the Immigrations Department for processing. Applicants shall keep a copy of the completed visa application file (including all translations and authentications) and bring the documents with them to the Dominican Republic to begin the process of the respective residency application.

3. Applicants then have 6 months (to avoid cancellation) to make the required trip to the city of Santo Domingo in the Dominican Republic for 2 business days for the processing of legal documentation, signing the appropriate application forms, registering their fingerprints, and the taking of a mandatory government medical test (1 of 2).

Provisional Residency
(Naturalization Only)

1. <u>**DAY 1**</u>: Under Immigration Department requirements, Applicants are required to pre-authorize the medical tests. Upon such authorization, a medical appointment will be scheduled on the following business day.

2. <u>**Day 2**</u>: Applicants 11 years of age and older shall be escorted by a representative of our provider law firm to appear at the Immigrations Department Medical Clinic at 08:00 hours for the following tests. Shoes must be worn (no sandals). Shorts, sleeveless shirts and blouses are prohibited. The entire examination, with travel time, generally takes 4 hours to complete. (Blood and Urine Sample / Chest X-Ray)

3. Upon completion of the aforementioned medical examination, Applicants are free to go.

4. In approximately 2 weeks, upon receipt of the medical test results, an application will be submitted to the Immigrations Department by our provider law firm with the following prepared documents. (Certificate of Good Behavior / Completed Application forms)

5. All documentation (original or copied) which are submitted to Immigrations shall become part of the Dominican Republic government file and will not be returned to Applicants.

6. Once applications have been submitted to Immigrations, the internal processing and investigation methods of the Immigrations Department is completely private and Applicants shall receive no further application information until the application has been approved, rejected or more Applicant information is required.

7. In approximately 6 months Applicants shall be contacted upon the decision reached by Immigrations to approve or reject the Applicants application.

8. Once approved, Applicants shall return to the city of Santo Domingo for 1 to 2 business days to accept the National ID Card (*Cedulà de Identidad Personal*) and Provisional Residency Card. (Passports must remain valid for at least 18 months to return to the DR)

9. Applicants choosing to reside in the Dominican Republic may begin to live and work at this time anywhere in the Dominican Republic for a period of 1 year. Resident Applicants have no further requirements to exit or re-enter the Dominican Republic during the remainder of the entire Citizenship and Passport process. Only legal residents may work in the DR.

10. During the first 6 months of Provisional Residency, Applicants may bring household goods into the Dominican Republic duty free.

Permanent Residency
(Naturalization / Investor / Rentista / Retiree)

1. In 1 year's time when the Provisional Residency Card is within 45 days of expiring, Applicants may apply for a Permanent Residency Card which is valid for 1 year, and renewable every 4 years thereafter. If, after 10 years, citizenship is not desired a 'Definitive Residency Card' is issued and an annual residency fee shall continue to be paid.

2. Applicants are required to return to Santo Domingo for 2 business days for the processing of legal documentation and the taking of a mandatory government medical test (2 of 2).

3. Applicants shall appear at the law offices of our legal provider and present the following documents.
   ‣ **Passport** (Current with no less than 18 months time before expiration)
   ‣ **National ID Card** (*Cedulà de Identidad Personal* issued previously by the Dominican Republic government)
   ‣ **Residency Card** (Issued previously by the Dominican Republic government)
   ‣ **Conditions Document** (Justifying that the conditions under which residency was originally granted have not changed, such as employment, investments, pensions, or change of address)

4. Applicants 11 years of age and older shall be escorted by a representative of our provider law firm to appear at the Immigrations Department Medical Clinic at 08:00 hours for the following tests. Shoes must be worn (no sandals). Shorts, sleeveless shirts and blouses are prohibited. The entire examination, with travel time, generally takes 4 hours to complete. (Blood Sample / Urine Sample / Chest X-Ray)

5. Upon completion of the aforementioned medical examination, Applicants are free to go.

6. In approximately 6 months Applicants shall be contacted and informed upon arrival of the Permanent Residency Card.

7. Applicants are required to return to Santo Domingo for one business day to accept the National ID Card (*Cedulà de Identidad Personal*) and Permanent Residency Card.

8. Upon acceptance of the National ID and Residency Cards, Applicants are free to go.

9. In exactly 1 year's time when the Permanent Residency Card expires, Applicants may apply for the Renewal of the Permanent Residency Card, which is then valid for and renewable every 4 years. Permanent Residents may apply for citizenship after only 2 years. Investors and spouses of Dominican national may apply after only 6 months.

Citizenship with Passport
(Naturalization / Investor / Rentista / Retiree)

1. Within 45 days of the Provisional or Permanent Residency Card expiration date, respective Applicants are required to return to the city of Santo Domingo for 2 to 3 business days to process legal documentation and accept the newly renewed National ID Card (*Cedulà de Identidad Personal*) and Permanent Residency Card.

2. Applicants shall appear at the law offices of our legal provider and present the following documents.
    ‣ **Passport** (Current with no less than six (6) months time before expiration)
    ‣ **National ID Card** (*Cedulà de Identidad Personal* issued previously by the Dominican Republic government)
    ‣ **Residency Card** (Issued previously by the Dominican Republic government)

3. Upon submission and same-day acceptance of the newly renewed National ID Card (*Cedulà de Identidad Personal*) and Permanent Residency Card, Applicants shall provide the following documentation to our provider law firm while still in the Dominican Republic.
    ‣ **Original Birth Certificate** duly translated in Spanish and apostilled from the issuing country of birth or authenticated from a Dominican Consulate
    ‣ **2 Color Copies of the Applicant's Passport**
    ‣ **Eight Passport Photos** (2" x 2") with four 4 and 4 right-hand side profiles. White background required and any accessories such as jewelry or sunglasses, etc are prohibited
    ‣ **Newly Renewed Permanent Residency Card**

4. The aforementioned documents provided by Applicants shall be combined and with the following document by our provider law firm and given to the Dominican Republic *"Ministerio de Interior y Policìa"*.
    ‣ **Affidavit of Solvency** of the guarantor backed by evidence of solvency (bank deposits or property titles) signed before a Dominican Notary or at Dominican Consulate

5. Applicants shall be provided questions and answers (pdf format) to study for their Spanish interview with the Dominican Republic *""Ministerio de Interior y Policìa"*.

6. The following day Applicants shall be escorted by a representative of our provider law firm to appear at the Dominican Republic *"Ministerio de Interior y Policìa"* for the Spanish interview.

7. Upon completion of the aforementioned Spanish interview, Applicants are free to go.

8. In approximately 3 to 5 months Applicants are required to return to the city of Santo Domingo for 1 to 2 business days for the Oath Ceremony.

9. Applicants shall be escorted by a representative of our provider law firm to appear for the Oath Ceremony to take the Dominican Republic Oath, which shall later be signed by the President of the Dominican Republic.

10. Upon completion of the aforementioned Oath Ceremony, Applicants are free to go.

11. Applicants are required to return to the city of Santo Domingo for 1 to 2 business days for the processing of legal documents.

12. Applicants shall appear at our provider law offices to receive their original Dominican Republic Birth Certificate and to be escorted to the Dominican Republic *"Ministerio de Interior y Policìa"* to receive a Naturalization Certificate and a new Dominican ID Card.

13. Applicants (now Citizens) shall be assisted with the DR Passport application process.

14. Citizens are required to return to the city of Santo Domingo for 1 to 2 business days for the processing of legal documentation and required banking deposit.

15. Applicants shall be escorted by a representative of our provider law firm to appear at the *"Banco de Reservas"* to pay taxes in the amount of RD$4,650 for the Passport to be available within 1 business week or RD$5,650 for the Passport to be available on the same business day.

16. Applicants shall be escorted by a representative of our provider law firm to appear at the *"Direcciòn General de Pasaportes"* before 12:00 PM with the following documents.
    ‣ **Naturalization Certificate**, issued by the DR *"Ministerio de Interior y Policìa"*
    ‣ **Original and Color Copy of the National ID Card for Citizens** (*Cedulà de Identidad*)
    ‣ **2 Passport Photos** (2" x 2") with 4 front and 4 right-hand side profiles. White background required and any accessories such as jewelry or sunglasses, etc are prohibited
    ‣ Original and Color Copy of the **Receipt of Payment** at the *"Banco de Reservas"*
    ‣ Original and Color Copy of the **Dominican Republic Birth Certificate**, duly legalized by the Junta Central Electoral (issued within the pervious 12 months)

17. Passport shall be available later the same day, if the *Direcciòn General de Pasaportes's* "VIP" fee is paid.

18. Upon completion of the aforementioned document processing, Citizens are free to go.

Provisional Residency

Residency Application*

- ✅ Dominican Republic Provisional Residency Application
- ✅ Dominican Republic 18% Service Tax
- ✅ Dominican Republic Government Fees and Expenses *($735)*
- ✅ Per Person *(Minimum 1 Adult Age 18+ Years Old)*
- ✅ Personal Assistance for Medical Tests
- ✅ Escort to Immigrations Department Medical Clinic
- ✅ Blood Sample / Urine Sample / Chest X-Ray
- ✅ Filing of Apostilled Personal Documents and Immigrations Department Documents
- ✅ Birth Certificate *(Original)*
- ✅ Marriage Certificate and University Degree *(If Applicable)*
- ✅ Certificate of "No Criminal Record"
- ✅ Eight (8) Passport Photos
- ✅ Color Copy of Passport with D.R. Visa Stamp
- ✅ Notarized Letter of Guarantee and Affidavit of Solvency
- ✅ Certificate of Good Behavior
- ✅ Submission of Completed Application Forms
- ✅ For Government Approved Applicants
- ✅ Provisional Residency Card *(Good for 1 Year)*
- ✅ Dominican Republic National ID Card *(Cédula)*
- ✅ Time to Provisional Residency is 6 Months
- ❌ Services are exclusive of any travel or travel related expenses to any Dominican Republic Consulate or the capital city of Santo Domingo in the Dominican Republic

Residency Renewals*

- ✅ Dominican Republic Provisional Residency Renewal
- ✅ Dominican Republic 18% Service Tax
- ✅ Dominican Republic Government Fees and Expenses *($514)*

* **Legal Fees** Please contact our offices for specific details.

Permanent Residency

Residency Application*

✅ Dominican Republic Permanent Residency Application

✅ Dominican Republic 18% Service Tax

✅ Dominican Republic Government Fees and Expenses *($475)*

✅ Per Person *(Minimum 1 Adult Age 18+ Years Old)*

✅ Personal Assistance for Medical Tests

✅ Escort to Immigrations Department Medical Clinic

✅ Blood Sample / Urine Sample / Chest X-Ray

✅ Filing of all Immigrations Department Documents

✅ Color Copy of Passport with D.R. Visa Stamp

✅ Dominican Republic Provisional Residency Card *(Previously Issued)*

✅ Dominican Republic National ID Card or Cédula *(Previously Issued)*

✅ For Government Approved Applicants

✅ Permanent Residency Card
   (Good for 1 Year and Renewable Every 4 Years Thereafter)

❌ Services are exclusive of any travel or travel related expenses to any Dominican Republic Consulate or the capital city of Santo Domingo in the Dominican Republic

Residency Renewals*

✅ Dominican Republic Permanent Residency Renewal

✅ Dominican Republic 18% Service Tax

✅ Dominican Republic Government Fees and Expenses *($543)*

* **Legal Fees** Please contact our offices for specific details.

Citizenship with Passport

Complete Application*

- Dominican Republic Citizenship with Passport
- Dominican Republic 18% Service Tax
- Dominican Republic Government Fees and Expenses *($1,688)*
- Per Person *(Minimum 1 Adult Age 18 Years of Age)*
- Filing of Apostilled Personal Documents Including:
- Birth Certificate *(Original)*
- Color Copy of Passport with D.R. Visa Stamp
- Eight (8) Passport Photos
- Filing of all Immigrations Department Documents
- Permanent Residency Card *(Previously Issued)*
- Dominican Republic National ID Card *(Cédula)*
- Filing of all Ministry of Interior Documents
- Affidavit of Solvency
- Personal Assistance for Spanish Interview
- Escorted to the "Ministerio de Interior y Policia"
- Personal Assistance for Oath Ceremony
- Escort to Oath Ceremony
- For Government Approved Applicants
- Original Dominican Republic Birth Certificate
- Dominican Republic Naturalization Certificate
- Dominican Republic ID Card for Citizens
- Expedited *(Required)* Passport Taxes
- Dominican Republic Passport
- ❌ Services are exclusive of any travel or travel related expenses to any Dominican Republic Consulate or the capital city of Santo Domingo in the Dominican Republic

* **Legal Fees** Please contact our offices for specific details.

St Kitts & Nevis

The Citizenship by Investment program is sanctioned by the government of St Kitts & Nevis and has been in existence since 1984 making it one of the most well-established programs of its kind in the world. St Kitts & Nevis citizens are allowed to hold dual citizenship and the acquisition of such citizenship is not reported to any other countries. Passports issued from St Kitts & Nevis enable visa-free travel to more than 125 countries and territories worldwide including the European Union and the United Kingdom. Although the government of St Kitts & Nevis has ceased granting Citizenship by Investment directly to Iranian residents, applications from Iranian citizens holding residency in another jurisdiction shall be accepted. Full citizenship in St Kitts & Nevis may be enjoyed for a lifetime and passed on to future generations by decent. St Kitts & Nevis citizens are not liable for any personal taxation whatsoever as there are no capital gains tax, no gift tax, no income tax, no inheritance tax and no wealth tax. Economic Citizenship can be obtained in St Kitts & Nevis through either the purchase of real property in a government 'approved project' in excess of $400,000 USD plus the applicable government fees, or through a one-time charitable contribution to the Sugar Industry Diversification Foundation (or SIDF) beginning at $250,000 USD inclusive of government fees.

St Kitts & Nevis
Economic Citizenship

In Association With

The Grant, Powell & Company law firm is the official corporate service provider of APSI for all incorporation and dual citizenship services within the jurisdiction of St Kitts & Nevis. APSI consulting services are inclusive within existing Grant, Powell & Company fees. There are absolutely no price increases whatsoever for our consulting services.

Grant, Powell & Company is a full-service law firm located in the capital city of Basseterre, St Kitts specializing in Asset Protection and Dual Citizenship services. Evolving through a succession of law firms dating back to 1990, Grant, Powell & Company is established as one of the leading private practice law firms in the twin island nation of St. Kitts & Nevis with licensed attorneys providing services as Barristers-at-Law and Solicitors.

Attorneys

Lindsay Grant

Lindsay obtained his undergraduate law degree (LLB) with honors from the University of the West Indies Cave Hill in Barbados, a Legal Education Certificate (LEC) from the Norman Manley Law School in Jamaica, and a Master in Laws (LLM) from Harvard University in Boston, Massachusetts.

Lindsay is an avid sportsman and has played cricket and football at the 1st division level. Lindsay was President of the St. Thomas Parish Football Association, President of the St. Kitts Cricket Association, and a National Table Tennis player.

A lawyer by profession, Lindsay lives and works in the Caribbean twin island nation of St. Kitts & Nevis. A former Vice-President, Secretary, and Treasurer of the St. Kitts & Nevis Bar Association, Lindsay has practiced law in St. Kitts & Nevis for 23 years.

- St. Kitts & Nevis Bar Association
- Organization of Eastern Caribbean States Bar Association
- International Trade Mark Association

Jonel Powell

Jonel obtained his undergraduate law degree (LLB) from the University of the West Indies Cave Hill in Barbados and a Legal Education Certificate (LEC) from the Norman Manley Law School in Jamaica. Before becoming a partner of Grant, Powell & Company, Jonel worked in the British Overseas Territory of Anguilla for a number of years. There he practiced Offshore Law, Commercial Law and Corporate Litigation with two of that jurisdiction's most prominent law firms.

A lawyer by profession, Jonel lives and works in the Caribbean twin island nation of St. Kitts & Nevis.

- St. Kitts & Nevis Bar Association
- Anguilla Bar Association
- Organization of Eastern Caribbean States Bar Association
- Rotary International

Grant, Powell & Company is a State Capital Global Law Firm Group Member Firm (with 140 top law firms comprised of over 11,500 attorneys in 80 countries worldwide), the International Trademark Association, and the St. Kitts & Nevis Chamber of Industry and Commerce.

Law License

SAINT CHRISTOPHER AND NEVIS

LICENCE ON BUSINESS AND OCCUPATIONS
(No. 6 of 1972)

FORM OF LICENCE

121210001

LINDSAY GRANT & JONEL POWELL

owner of

GRANT, POWELL & CO

#3 CHURCH STREET BASSETERRE

having paid the annual Business and Occupation Licence fee is
hereby licensed to carry on the business of

LAWYERS

This licence expires on the 31st day of December 2013

This licence is not transferable to any other person or entity.

ISSUED THIS 06 DAY OF FEBUARY 2013

for Minister of Finance

ISSUED AT   BASSETERRE   06-FEB-2013 11:15:28 AM
THIS CERTIFICATE IS INVALID WITHOUT MINISTER OF FINANCE SIGNATURE AND THE SEAL OF THE INLAND REVENUE DEPARTMENT.

Certificate of Authorization

Saint Christopher and Nevis

FINANCIAL SERVICES REGULATORY COMMISSION

Certificate of Authorisation

No. 241

I hereby Certify that

GRANT, POWELL & CO.

has satisfied the requirements for the granting of authorisation under the The Financial Services
(Regulations) Order Cap 21.03 (Seventh Schedule) and is accordingly a person duly authorised
to carry on Corporate Business from the 1st day of February 2013 until the 31st day of
December 2013 in or from within the isle of Saint Christopher.

Granted this 8th day of February, 2013 at Saint
Christopher and Nevis.

Financial Services Regulatory Commission

Foreword

1st August 2013

Mr Jay Butler
Via Soldini I4
Chaisso
Ticino
6830 Switzerland (CH)

Dear Mr Bulter,

This is an opportune time to publicly acknowledge with appreciation, your work in the area of Economic Citizenship. Your experience and wealth of knowledge in the subject matter is clearly evident in this publication, which no doubt will make a meaningful contribution to literature in the field. The book is user friendly and will serve as an excellent resource for a wide range of stakeholders. I take this opportunity to congratulate you on this accomplishment.

Wishing you continued success.

Kindest regards

Lindsay F. P. Grant LLB (Hons), LEC, LLM (Harvard)
Senior Partner
GRANT, POWELL & CO

GRANT, POWELL & CO.

BARRISTERS-AT-LAW & SOLICITORS

TRADEMARK & PATENT AGENTS

NOTARIES PUBLIC

PARTNERS

LINDSAY F.P. GRANT
LLB (HONS), LEC, LLM (HARVARD)

JONEL F.H. POWELL
LLB (HONS), LEC

P.O. Box 823

#3 Church Street

Basseterre, St. Kitts, W.I.

Tel: (869) 465 - 3673 /

(516) - 320 - 6695

Fax: (869) 466 - 3854

Email: info@grantpowellandco.com

Web: www.grantpowellandco.com

STATE CAPITAL GROUP
GLOBAL CONNECTIONS. LEGAL SOLUTIONS

Member firms of the State Capital Group practice independently and not in a relationship for the joint practice of law.

About St Kitts & Nevis

Activities

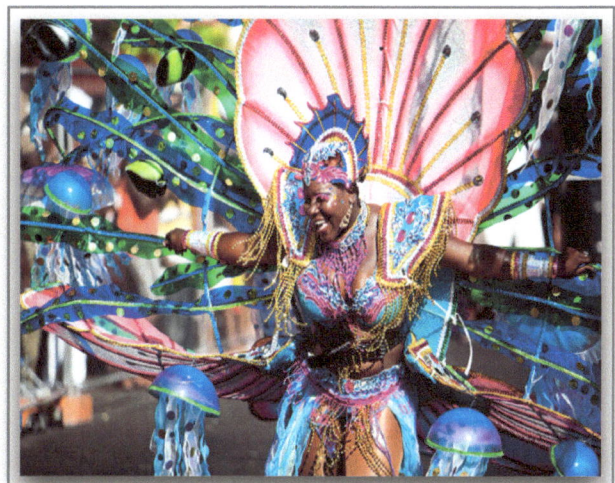

The twin-island nation of St. Kitts & Nevis offers a wide array of outdoor activities. Nevis invites visitors to the Botanical Gardens, an 11 mile hike up Nevis Peak, snorkeling at Oualie, and relaxing on 3-mile long Pinney's Beach. St. Kitts has a scenic railway, beautiful arts and crafts unique to the country, plantation home tours, and the famous Brimestone Hill Fortress. Together the islands provide deep sea fishing, world renowned golfing, hiking, hot springs, mountain biking, ocean kayaking, para-sailing, scuba diving, swimming, windsurfing, and more.

Climate

St. Kitts & Nevis enjoys a tropical marine climate with a typical wet and dry season. Northeasterly trade winds and regional oceanic cyclones can have a profound influence on the local weather patterns. Generally the islands have warm and consistent temperatures averaging 24°C to 27°C with a humidity rate of only 71%. Rainfall levels increase with altitude as annual precipitation ranges from 40 cm in the coastal areas to 152 cm in the central mountains. The moderate rainy season is considered to last from May to October, with the heaviest accumulations occurring during July and August.

Culture

The culture of St. Kitts & Nevis could best be described as festive and vibrant with a variety of carnivals and outdoor celebrations taking place throughout the year. Over 50% of the country is actively religious and the primary denomination is Catholic. Christmas in particular is an extremely social time of year with the Carnival Masquerade, the National Carnival Queen Pageant, the Miss Caribbean Talented Teen Pageant, and the Junior Calypso Show. In the summer the island of St. Kitts hosts a musical festival including jazz, salsa, soca, calypso, and steelpan music. In keeping with the "Pirates of the Caribbean" spirit, St. Kitts & Nevis is known for its rum manufacturing distilled from local sugar cane.

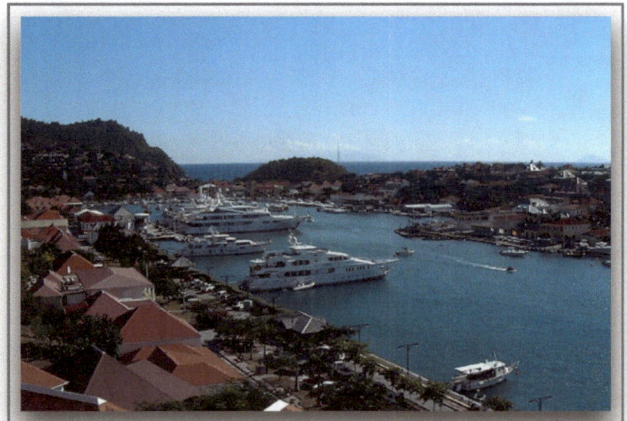

Economy and Offshore Financial Services

The economy of St. Kitts & Nevis traditionally lied within the sugar cane industry, however tourism, manufacturing, salt mining, and offshore banking have replaced a large percentage of the overall economy. Although 39% of the total land area is devoted to crops (the two primary crops are sugar cane and peanuts), the vast majority of produce and poultry is required to be imported along with key energy resources such as natural gas and oil. Local harvests of sweet potatoes, onions, tomatoes, cabbage, carrots, and fish help supply the community, but the demand for agricultural products and common staple goods require scheduled imports from the U.S and Canada. St. Kitts and Nevis is a member of the Eastern Caribbean Currency Union (ECCU), the Eastern Caribbean Central Bank (ECCB), and the Eastern Caribbean Telecommunications (ECTEL) Authority. Asset Protection Services of America offers the St. Kitts & Nevis citizenship by investment program as well as incorporation services for Business Companies, Citizenship by Investment, Foundations, International Exempt Trusts and Limited Liability Companies.

Geography

St. Kitts & Nevis is located in the Leeward Islands in the West Indies and has a total land mass of just 270 square kilometers. Saint Kitts is a longitudinal island at 180 square kilometers while the smaller island Nevis, which sits 3 kilometers to the south of St. Kitts, has a total land mass of 93 square kilometers. Both islands are comprised primarily of volcanic rock. The virtually round island of Nevis features the highest national point that is a dormant volcano called Mount Liamuiga at 1,156 meters above sea level. St. Kitts is home to a 270 acre great salt pond natural preserve for a wide range of biodiversity.

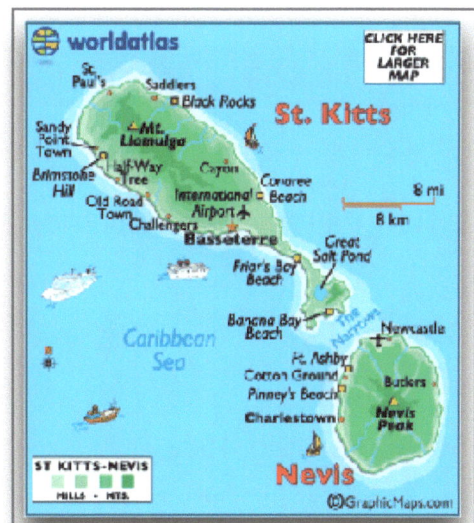

History

The islands of St. Kitts & Nevis were alleged to have been first spotted by Christopher columbus in 1493. In time the islands became known to ship captains for their fresh water, fertile soil, and large salt deposits. In 1624 the colony of Saint Christopher became the first English colony in the Caribbean. One year later the French joined the English colony in an attempt to out-populate the local Kalinago, whom had grown suspicious of the of the foreign presence. Such suspicion proved accurate as the combined English and French forces committed genocide murdering over 2,000 Kalinago men. Their bodies were dumped into a river where the blood was said to flow for days giving rise to the name "Bloody River". The few remaining Kalinago Indians were then deported. The islands remained a strategic military outpost for centuries and a central location of slave labor to harvest tobacco, sugar cane and salt. The French, English and Spanish fought over control of the islands until the Treaty of Ultrecht was signed in 1713, which ceded St. Kitts to the British in perpetuity.

Interesting Facts

Capital Basseterre	Population 60,000
Official Language English	GDP $557 Million
Government Unitary Parliamentary Republic	Currency East Caribbean Dollar
Laws Common Law	Driving Left
Independence Day September 19th, 1983	Internet .kn
Total Area 261 Km2	Calling Code +1 (869)

Constitution of St Kitts & Nevis

Upon resolution for termination of association with the United Kingdom, the Constitution of St. Kitts & Nevis was drafted, passed in the House of Assembly, and came into operation June 23rd, 1983. Regarding citizenship, the constitution states in part.

Chapter VIII, Citizenship (Section 94)
Acquisition, Renunciation, Certification and Deprivation

(94) There shall be such provision as may be made by Parliament-
   a) for naturalization as citizens of person who are not entitled to become citizens under Section 92

Such provision by Parliament is the "Citizenship by Investment" program established under the Citizenship Act the following year in 1984.

Citizenship Act, 1984

Part II (Section 3, Part 5)

"Subject to subsections (8) and (9) of this section, a person is entitled, upon making application under this subsection to the Minister in the prescribed manner and upon payment of any fee that may be prescribed, to be registered as a citizen of St. Christopher and Nevis without any rights of voting save under and in accordance with the provisions of any law governing the qualifications of voters, if the Cabinet is satisfied that such person has invested substantially in St. Christopher and Nevis."

Diplomatic Relations

St. Kitts & Nevis enjoys stable diplomatic relations with most countries worldwide and holds membership in the United Nations, the Organization of the Americas (OAS), the World Trade Organization (WTO), the Organization of Eastern Caribbean States (OECS), the Eastern Caribbean Economic Union (ECEU), and the Caribbean Community (CARICOM). Citizenship in St. Kitts & Nevis affords the right to take up residence in St. Kitts & Nevis as well as other member countries within the Caribbean Community at any time or for any length of time.

1.) Antigua and Barbuda	9.) Jamaica
2.) Bahamas	10.) Montserrat
3.) Barbados	11.) Saint Lucia
4.) Belize	12.) St. Kitts & Nevis
5.) Commonwealth of Dominica	13.) St. Vincent & the Grenadines
6.) Grenada	14.) Suriname
7.) Guyana	15.) Trinidad and Tobago
8.) Haiti	

Documents

Economic citizenship applicants need to provide the following particulars:

1.) Police record from current resident jurisdiction. (Minors need not provide a police record.)
2.) An HIV test which must come from a lab, not a just a medical practitioner. (Minors need not provide an HIV test.)
3.) Four (4) Passport size photos.
4.) Notarized, full-color copy of the picture page of your passport with particulars.
5.) Notarized Original Birth Certificate
6.) Notarized Original Marriage Certificate
7.) If Divorced, Notarized Original Divorce Decree.
8.) Affidavit of Support (Grant, Powell & Co. will assist you with this)
9.) Proof Residency (Notarized color-copy of a utility bill, etc)
10.) Consent form to be provided by the head of the household; such form must be signed by all parties over the age of eighteen (18) years of age.
11.) Job Reference Letter (If Applicable)

Incorporation Services

The Gibraltar Trust Company is a wholly-owned subsidiary of the Grant, Powell and Company law firm and, in conjunction with Asset Protection Services of America, provides complete incorporation services in St Kitts & Nevis for Business Corporations, Foundations, Trusts and Limited Liability Companies.

Gibraltar Trust Company

Property

Island Realty and Property Management is a wholly-owned subsidiary of the Grant, Powell and Company law firm and a licensed real estate firm in St. Kitts & Nevis. An ideal company for helping locate the right property in an "Approved Project", Island Realty and Property Management is a full service firm and can meet all your real estate investment needs. Their legal staff ensures your transaction runs smoothly during purchase, while their management services offer peace of mind handling all on-going rental, maintenance and repair of your investment after closing.

Taxation

St. Kitts & Nevis citizens and residents have no capital gains tax, no gift tax, no income tax, no inheritance tax and no wealth tax.

Visa-Free on Arrival

Andorra	Estonia	Korea	Somoa (Western)
Anguilla	Faroe Islands	Latvia	San Marino
Antigua & Barbuda	Fiji	Lesotho	Seychelles
Argentina	Finland	Liechtenstein	Singapore
Aruba	France	Lithuania	Slovakia
Austria	French Polynesia	Luxembourg	Slovenia
Bahamas	Georgia	Malawi	Spain
Barbados	Germany	Malaysia	St. Lucia
Belize	Gibraltar	Maldives	St. Vincent
Bermuda	Greece	Malta	Suriname
British Virgin Islands	Greenland	Mauritius	Sweden
Bulgaria	Grenada	Micronesia	Switzerland
Canada	Guatemala	Montserrat	Tanzania
Chile	Guyana	Netherlands	Trinidad & Tobago
Columbia	Haiti	Netherlands Antilles	Tunisia
Cook Islands	Honduras	Nicaragua	Turks & Caicos
Costa Rica	Hong Kong	Niue	United Kingdom
Croatia	Hungary	Norway	Vanuatu
Cuba	Iceland	Palestinian Territories	Vatican City
Cyprus	Ireland	Panama	Venezuela
Czech Republic	Israel	Peru	Zambia
Denmark	Italy	Philippines	Zimbabwe
Dominican Republic	Jamaica	Poland	
Ecuador	Kenya	Portugal	
El Salvador	Kiribati	Romania	

Visa on Arrival

Armenia	Jordan	Nepal	Tonga
Belarus	Laos	Palau Island	Turkey
Bolivia	Lebanon	Sierra Leone	Turkmenistan
Djibouti	Macau	Solomon Islands	
Egypt	Madagascar	Timor-Leste	
Gambia	Nauru	Togo	

Citizenship by Investment
Real Property

The first method of obtaining St Kitts & Nevis economic citizenship is by means of purchasing real property through a government approved project valued at $400,000 (USD) or more. Raw land may also be purchased under the Citizenship by Investment (CBI) program provided the value reaches or exceeds $700,000 in value. Investors or multiple parties may invest together into the purchase of a more expensive home or raw land so-long-as the aggregate amount of the property or land exceeds the aforementioned minimum requirements per household. Toward this end, some developers offer government approved (CBI) time-share properties.

Single Person $400,000*
- Government Due Diligence Fee *($7,500)*
- Government Application Form *($250)*
- Minimum Investment in Real Property *($400,000)*
- Legal Fees for Property Transfer *(1.5% of Sale Price established by Bar Association)*
- Property Assurance Fund *(0.2% Sale Price as Required by Law)*
- Government Citizenship Fees for 1 Adult *($50,000)*
- Survey Plans *($115)*
- Government Issued Passport *($350)*
- Certificate of Citizenship *($47)*
- Police Certificate *($10)*

Married Couple $495,250*
- Government Application Form *($250)*
- Government Citizenship Fees for Spouse *($25,000)*

Married Couple with Dependents $524,500*
- Government Application Form per Dependent *($250)*
- Government Due Diligence Fee *($4,000 per Additional Dependent)*
- Government Due Diligence Fee *($7,500 for the Head of Household)*
- Government Citizenship Fees *($25,000 Per Dependent Ages 0 to 17)*
- Government Citizenship Fees *($50,000 Per Dependent Ages 18 to 25)*

* Legal Fees Please contact our offices for specific details.

Citizenship by Investment
Sugar Industry Diversification Foundation (SIDF)

The second method of obtaining St Kitts & Nevis economic citizenship is by means of a charitable contribution to the SIDF (Sugar Industry Diversification Foundation). Families who were hardest-hit by changes in the global economy receive the funds in an effort to revitalize the community, to help once thriving sugar cane communities rebuild after repercussions from the 'artificial sweetener' industry. All Government fees are included in the below SIDF donation amounts.

Single Person $250,000*

Married Couple with Up to 1 Dependent Child $300,000*

Married Couple with Up to 3 Dependent Child $350,000*

Married Couple with Up to 5 Dependent Child $450,000*

Government Citizenship Fees for Each Additional Dependent Child $50,000*

Fees Applicable to All SIDF Programs
- Primary Government Fees *(Included in the respective donation amount)*
- Government Issued Passport *($350)*
- Certificate of Citizenship *($47)*
- Police Certificate *($10)*
- Government Application Form per Dependent *($250)*
- Government Due Diligence Fee *($4,000 per Additional Dependent)*
- Government Due Diligence Fee *($7,500 for the Head of Household)*

* Legal Fees Please contact our offices for specific details.

Approved Projects
Nevis

Busch Hill Garden Villas

Designed to provide elegant spaces in which to live, entertain and relax. Their spacious villas range from 168 m2 to 232 m2 of living space complete with a great room, fully equipped kitchen, air-conditioning, furniture package, and 3-4 bedrooms each with a private en-suite bathroom. Villas are constructed of highly durable modern materials resistant to insects and hurricanes. The property designs reflect traditional Caribbean architecture and styles with hip roofs and gingerbread.

Cliffdwellers

Cliffdwellers is a smaller luxury community nestled on 14 acres of land overlooking the Caribbean Sea. The resort has two distinct residential enclaves, the first being ten luxury villas built on a steep cliff (hence Cliffdwellers) and the second being fourteen condominiums situated on a gentle plain along the shoreline. All dwellings have access to a community beach house, boat house, fitness center, tennis courts, and direct beach access with swimming, snorkeling, shelling, fishing and boating.

Fern Hill Estates

The estates are nestled along 35 acres of prime hillside land in Nevis. The properties feature spacious verandas with spectacular panoramic views and grounds which support the organic growth of coconut palms, mangoes and tamarind. Secluded in a lush tropical forest, the area is filled with natural water courses, boulders, caves and exotic vegetation. The entire project is located only 1.5 miles from Pinneys Beach, a 10 minute drive to the capital of Charleston, and a 15 minute drive to the international airport.

Approved Projects
Nevis

The Four Seasons Resort Estates

In keeping with the acclaimed 5-star quality of Four Seasons hotels and resorts around the world, the custom estates in Nevis include a Robert Trent Jones II golf course, professional tennis complex, fitness center, and seaside restaurant. Private residences offer luxurious comfort and are surrounded by luscious gardens and far-reaching views. Some homes reflect Nevisian heritage with touches of gingerbread, balustrades and louvered shutters while others possess an air of simple contemporary sophistication.

The Hamilton at Nelson Spring

Located on the picturesque west coast of Nevis, the development contains 10 buildings on 6 acres of prime beachfront property with a combined total of 30 condominiums and two-story townhouses. With only a few exceptions, all the buildings are positioned to give each unit an ocean view. Amenities include a full-time management staff with 24-hour security, maintenance, house-keeping, babysitting, and a business center. Facilities include a centrally located community pool with swim-up bar, a state-of-the-art fitness center, all weather tennis court, tranquility garden, and a full service spa.

Approved Projects
St Kitts

Christophe Harbour

This full-scale luxury resort community features over 2,500 acres of land offering a complete range of outdoor adventures and includes multiple world-class resorts such as the Sandy Bank Bay Bungalows (Sold Out), the Windswept Residence Club (offering Fractional Ownership), Harbourside Properties, Cardinal Point, Whitehouse Bay, the Tom Fazio golf course (which hosts PGA tournaments), the Super Yacht Marina and Village (capable of holding 300+ foot yachts), the 5-star Park Hyatt Hotel, the Pavillion Beach Club and the Beach House (which rival any of the finest beach clubs in the Caribbean).

Kittitian Hill

Set on the gentle slope of Mount Liamuiga on the island of St. Kitts, Kittitian Hill is a unique luxury resort development which is sensitive to the environment and to the heritage and people of St. Kitts. The development incorporates unique architecture, landscape and interior designs of renowned architect Bill Bensley, known for his award winning resorts throughout South East Asia. Every property offers panoramic views of St. Barts. St. Eustatius, Saba, St. Martin, and dramatic views of the Caribbean Sea. Amenities include an 18-hole championship golf course designed by Ian Woosnam, a luxurious destination spa, and "The Village" where you can find an excellent selection of dining and entertainment options including bars, restaurants, duty free shops, cinema, library and amphitheater. This unique community is managed by Sedona Resorts, creator and operators of the world-renowned and award-winning Mii Amo Spa in Sedona, Arizona. Prices include furniture packages, stamp duties, and conveyance and survey fees.

Approved Projects
St Kitts

Ocean's Edge

This hillside property is located overlooking the North Frigate Bay with spectacular 180° views of the Atlantic Ocean. The development spans nearly 40 acres and, along with 46 private hilltop villas, contains 153 one, two, and three bedroom hillside apartments, 148 poolside residences, and 62 one and two bedroom beachfront apartments. Resort amenities include a beachfront bar and restaurant, clubhouse with restaurant, recreational center, communal swimming pools, tennis courts, and onsite concierge and housekeeping services.

Silver Reef

Located in the coveted Frigate Bay district, the property rests on a 4.6 acre natural rise overlooking the Atlantic coast to the left and the Caribbean Sea to the right. The gardens situated at the base of the units join to the fairways of the Royal St. Kitts Golf Course. Phase one of the development is complete and occupied with Phase Two set for completion in 2012. The development features three swimming pools set in natural landscaped gardens, one centrally located free form pool, while the beach is within 5 minutes walking distance.

Approved Projects
St Kitts

Sundance Ridge

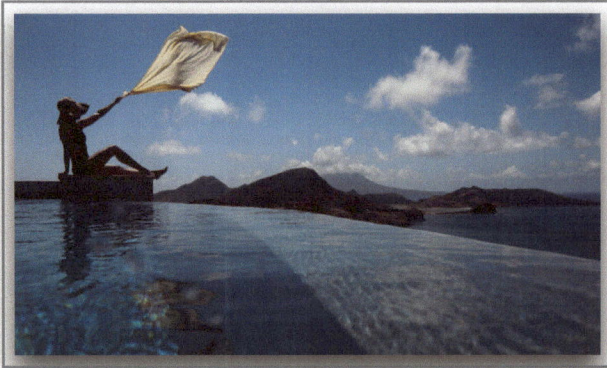

The developers of Sundance Ridge have collectively built over 100 premium villas on the island of St. Kitts and their world-class engineering, architecture and custom designs have culminated in this turn-key project. Sundance Ridge rises 150 meters above sea level on the narrow portions of the St. Kitts Southeast Peninsula. Each of the 15 custom built villas sits on a at least ½ acre of land featuring spectacular panoramic views from expansive outdoor verandas with infinity edge pools. Complete furniture packages can be based around your set budget, and the interior designs, amenities, appliances, cabinetry, and even the villas themselves are custom-driven to suit your tastes.

Sunrise Hills Villas

The Sunrise Hills Villas development is an approved project for the Citizenship by Investment program sanctioned by the government of St. Kitts & Nevis. The newly built units are available with spacious french doors leading onto a veranda overlooking uninterrupted views of the Royal St. Kitts Golf Course, a natural landscape of Frigate Bay, the St. Kitts coastline and Atlantic ocean. Villas includes all major appliances, off road parking, community tennis courts and a pool.

www.ingramcontent.com/pod-product-compliance
Lightning Source LLC
Chambersburg PA
CBHW041449210326
41599CB00004B/192